Taxcafe.co.uk Tax Guides

Incorporate and Save Tax

By Lee Hadnum LLB ACA CTA

Important Legal Notices:

TAXCafe™
TAX GUIDE - "Incorporate and Save Tax"

Published by:
Taxcafe UK Limited
4 Polwarth Gardens
Edinburgh EH11 1LW
Tel: (0044) 01592 560081

Email: team@taxcafe.co.uk

First Edition, August 2003
Second Edition, March 2004

ISBN 1 904608 11 6

Disclaimer

Before reading or relying on the content of this Tax Guide please read
carefully the disclaimer at the end of the guide. If you have any queries
then please contact the publisher at team@taxcafe.co.uk.

About the Author

Lee Hadnum is a key member of the Taxcafe.co.uk team. Apart from authoring a number of our tax guides, he also provides personalised tax advice through our popular Question & Answer Service, a role he carries out with a great deal of enthusiasm and professionalism.

Lee is a rarity among tax advisers having both legal AND chartered accountancy qualifications. After qualifying as a prize winner in the Institute of Chartered Accountants entrance exams, he went on to become a Chartered Tax Adviser (CTA).

Having worked in Ernst & Young's tax department for a number of years, Lee decided to start his own tax consulting firm, specialising in capital gains tax, inheritance tax and business tax planning.

He also tutors at a number of accountancy colleges in the north-west of England.

Whenever he has spare time Lee enjoys DIY, walking and travelling.

If you would like further advice, Lee can be contacted directly at lee@taxcafe.co.uk

Nick Braun, Managing Director, Taxcafe UK Limited

Contents

Chapter 1

Introduction

It's a decision that could save you thousands of pounds in tax each year, maybe tens of thousands.

You'll probably have guessed that I'm referring to the tax benefits of "incorporation" - the horrible word accountants use to describe "starting a company".

So what's it all about? Well, UK businesses are made up of sole traders, partnerships and companies. You also get limited liability partnerships, companies limited by guarantee and other weird and wonderful business structures but they simply are not that important from a tax angle.

Sole traders and partnerships have one key thing in common: they are unincorporated businesses. This means all the profits are added to the owner's or partner's other income and subject to income tax.

A company is, by contrast, separate from its owners (the shareholders) and is subject to its very own tax regime: Corporation tax.

So why incorporate?

Unlike other self-employed people, shareholder/directors are in the fortunate position of wearing two caps. On the one hand,

they can reward their hard work as an employee. On the other, they can reward their entrepreneurship as a shareholder.

As a company employee and shareholder you will be able to split your income into salary and dividends and this could generate large income tax and national insurance savings.

National insurance rates were increased significantly in the 2002 Budget so taking steps to eliminate this extra tax burden is more important than ever. And company owners have more scope than anyone else to carry out effective national insurance planning.

Another reason for trading through a company is to make the most of the currently low rates of corporation tax. The corporation tax regime has become more and more attractive in recent years and in some circumstances the first £10,000 of company profits can be tax free for a company, although the changes in the 2004 Budget effectively mean that many small owner managed companies will be paying corporation tax at a rate of 19%.

There was much speculation that the 2004 Budget would end the significant benefits of incorporation. However, the Budget has come and gone and, while there have been changes and the detailed interpretation of the provisions has yet to be put in place, by and large the opportunities to slash your tax bill are still there.

There are also many *non* tax reasons why using a company might be a good or even a bad idea. Many of these are listed below but they are not the focus of the guide. No other publication focuses on the all important tax benefits of incorporation, but there are plenty that focus on all the other issues.

Chapter 2

Non-tax Reasons for Using a Company

The most important reason for setting up a company is to save tax. However, there are many other benefits which have nothing to do with cutting your tax bill. Although these are not the focus of this guide, they are worth mentioning in brief:

Limited Liability Protection

In layman's language this means that a company's shareholders are not responsible for the company's debts and cannot be sued by outsiders.

This legal protection comes about because the company and its owners are separate legal entities in the eyes of the law.

In practice, much of the limited liability benefit will be taken away by cautious lenders and suppliers. For example, banks will usually not lend your company any money without the directors/shareholders first providing personal guarantees. In fact, many banks make it compulsory to have the personal guarantee concept explained to you by a solicitor... which could cost you hundreds in legal fees.

There are also a number of laws that limit the usefulness of limited liability protection. For example, the wrongful trading legislation effectively states that a director is liable for the debts of a company, where he knows that the company is in a poor financial state yet continues to trade.

Having said this, limited liability protection could prove invaluable, especially if you receive a lawsuit out of the blue or the company goes bankrupt and creditors who did not ask for guarantees are beating at your door. In these circumstances you will owe nothing, except any remaining share capital unpaid.

Borrowing Money

It is potentially easier for a company to raise additional finance.

For example, an unincorporated business cannot raise a "floating charge" over its assets, a company can. (With a floating charge the lender's claim is lodged over a group of assets rather than one specific asset. This leaves the borrower free to sell, buy and vary the assets within the group.)

Equity finance is also available to companies, and there are schemes such as the Enterprise Investment Scheme ("EIS"), that can provide tax relief for the providers of the finance.

Enhanced Status

Trading as a company is often seen as more prestigious than trading in your own name. Many people will have more faith in a business called Joe Bloggs Limited than just plain Joe Bloggs. Of course it makes virtually no difference in practice whether a business is incorporated or not.

Flexibility of Ownership

Using a company makes it easy to involve new people in the ownership of the business and to separate ownership and management.
For example, if you want to involve your adult children or key employees, all you have to do is issue them some shares.

If you want to keep your stake in the business but do not want to be involved in its day to day management, you can hold onto your shares but resign as an employee.

Continuity

It's something almost nobody setting up a business thinks about but it's probably the most important decision facing business owners close to retirement: succession.

A company structure allows for a smooth exit from the company.

The death of a company member does not affect the existence of the company. If a partner dies the partnership ceases to exist.

Chapter 3

Company Drawbacks

Using a company is not always in your best interests and it's worth pointing out some of the negative factors:

Costs

It costs virtually nothing to set up a company. All you have to do is go to one of the many company formation experts and they'll do most of the work for little more than £100.

Where you will incur higher costs is in ongoing accountancy fees. Most accountants charge companies more than sole traders and partnerships because of the extra requirements to prepare and file accounts with Companies House. In most cases the tax savings should easily cover these extra fees.

Company Law

As a company director you will be subject to UK company law. Loans to directors are prohibited (apart from small loans of less than £5,000) and there are separate taxation rules that apply an additional tax charge of 25% of the amount of the loan. If the loan is repaid the tax charge is effectively repaid. This is discussed in more detail later in this guide.

Larger companies (those with gross annual income of more than £1 million) require an audit, which can be costly.

Reporting Requirements

When you operate as a company your annual accounts have to be filed with Companies House. These will reveal financial information about your company. However, small companies only need to file an abbreviated balance sheet. These documents will tell the outside world very little about your dealings.

Accounts must be filed within 10 months of the end of the financial year and there are penalties for late filing.

Company directors are also obliged to keep minutes of directors' meetings, and to comply with statutory filing obligations. Every year an annual return has to be filed with Companies House but, unless there have been significant changes to the company's ownership or structure, this is essentially a 10 minute exercise. There is a small annual filing fee of less than £20.

PAYE

PAYE applies to any business that has employees and can therefore apply to not just limited companies but also unincorporated businesses.

The difference with a company is that, for a sole trader business, the proprietor will not be an employee and therefore not subject to PAYE - rather he or she will be taxed on the profits of the business.

In a limited company setting, the chances are that the directors (previously the sole trader and often a spouse) will also be employees and therefore PAYE would be deducted from any salaries paid to them.

PAYE is essentially a method of paying income tax throughout the year, and the employer company will therefore need to calculate the appropriate income tax and national insurance to deduct from any salary payments and pay this over to Inland Revenue.

PAYE is usually paid over on a monthly basis: every month you pay the income tax and national insurance for the previous month. However where the monthly income tax and national insurance is less than £1,500, quarterly payments are permitted.

In order to start paying PAYE, the first thing to do is phone Inland Revenue's new employer helpline. They will send you a "starter pack" that explains how PAYE is deducted, along with a variety of forms for you to use. An even better idea is to get a bean counter to do it for you!

Chapter 4

Why You & The Company Aren't Really Separate

This is the shortest chapter in this guide but the message is an important one.

Although you and your company are separate legal entities, it always amazes us how many authors write about companies and their owner/managers as if they were truly separate. What nonsense!

As a company owner you care very much about how the company's money is spent. It is in reality - no matter what the textbooks say - YOUR money. As a shareholder you have the ultimate say as to whether it goes to pay for your holiday or is simply given away to charity. Nobody else can tell you what to do with the company's money except in very exceptional circumstances. In practice, therefore, you and your company are not really separate.

Why are we even mentioning this? Because throughout this guide when we compare the tax treatment of companies and unincorporated businesses we are interested in the **whole** picture. We do not just look at the company's tax position in isolation from you the owner/employee. We also do not look at your personal tax in isolation from the company's tax bill. We look at both as a single unit. This is the only way to compare doing business through a company with doing business as a sole trader or partnership.

Doing something that decreases your personal tax bill is not much use if it has an adverse effect on the company's tax position. It's your company so in reality the company's tax bill is your tax bill.

Although there are special tax and other laws that affect you and the company differently, ultimately your aim is to use these to best advantage to improve your personal financial position.

There are many detailed examples of tax savings in this guide. Note that all of these examples take into account the tax position of both the company and its owners. So we may be including many taxes in the mix: corporation tax, income tax, capital gains tax and national insurance.

Chapter 5

Company Tax: Pros & Cons

Before taking a detailed look at how companies are taxed and how these special laws can be put to good use to cut your tax bill, it is worth briefly listing the tax benefits of doing business through a company:

The Pros

- Corporation tax rates are generally much lower than income tax rates. For example a company with profits of up to £300,000 will pay tax at a rate of just 19%.

- The maximum marginal tax rate for companies is only 32.75%, compared with 40% for sole traders and partnerships.

- Company directors can pay themselves a mix of salary and dividends that produces the lowest possible tax bill.

- Further income splitting can be achieved if your spouse is also a shareholder.

- There is no national insurance to pay on your dividends.

- Corporation tax is generally paid nine months after the end of the company's accounting period (although for certain "large" companies with profits above £1.5 million, payments on account are required during the accounting period). Compare this with income tax which sole traders have to pay twice yearly on 31 January and 31 July.

And the Cons ...

- There is a potential double tax charge on assets sold by the company. First corporation tax has to be paid by the company, then income tax has to be paid by the shareholders if the funds are taken out of the company.

- Sole traders and business partners enjoy "business asset" taper relief when they make capital gains from selling "trading assets". Potentially 75 per cent of the profits are tax free after just two years.

  Companies are not so fortunate. Instead they get Indexation Relief which simply protects that part of their capital gain which is inflationary - 2 or 3 per cent per year in the current low inflation climate. All is not lost, however, as company shareholders do enjoy the full business asset taper relief if they sell their shares in the company rather than the asset itself.

- Companies do not enjoy an annual capital gains tax allowance.

- Companies are subject to a separate regime for the taxation of interest. Special regulations govern loans to or from the company, which can cause frustration.

Chapter 6

Corporation Tax in Plain English

The most important difference between the way companies and other businesses are taxed can be summarised as follows:

Sole traders/partners pay <u>income tax</u> on their profits and <u>capital gains tax</u> on their capital gains.

Companies pay <u>corporation tax</u> on both their income and capital gains.

In this section we will show you how corporation tax is calculated. Despite all the mumbo-jumbo in tax textbooks, it's actually quite simple. We will also use a number of examples to compare income tax with corporation tax. The differences are potentially enormous.

6.1 Trading v Investment

First of all we must explain the differences between a **trading company** and an **investment company**. There are some key differences in the tax treatment of each. In layman's language, a trading company is a "regular" business such as a firm of graphic designers or a restaurant or a car dealership. These types of business are the focus of this guide. An investment company is a company which obtains the majority of its income from holding investments such as property.

It can be difficult to distinguish between trading and investment. However, where the business involves passively holding assets, this will be regarded as an investment activity. Common examples of this include a company letting property or receiving dividends or interest from another group company.

As we said, this guide focuses on trading companies. Why? Because one of the key tax issues when incorporating an *existing* business is whether capital gains tax can be avoided when the business is transferred into the company. In general only trading businesses can defer capital gains tax when they incorporate. An investment business may face a significant tax bill on incorporation.

Note that when you incorporate your business, you will receive a form from the Inland Revenue asking for details of the company (eg its activities and its accounting period end date) and details of the shareholders.

In addition, from 1 April 2004, you will also have to notify the Inland Revenue within three months of the date that you start trading – it is the date that you start trading that your accounting period for tax purposes begins.

6.2 Corporation Tax Rates

The taxable profits of a company are calculated in a similar way to a sole trader/partnership. The starting point is "accounting profit" and amounts are then added or subtracted from this figure to calculate taxable profit.

A simple example of how accounting profits differ from taxable profits is computer spending. In your tax return you can claim a 50% allowance for assets purchased between 1 April 2004 and 31 March 2005, yet in your accounts you might write the asset off over 5 years, with a 20% allowance in year one. Clearly the taxable profits would then be lower than the accounting profits.

Another similarity is that companies and other businesses are both subject to different tax rates as their profits increase.

Although both companies and other businesses pay tax at a higher rate as their profits increase, company tax rates are generally much lower than income tax rates. For companies the rates were changed in the Budget for the 2002 financial year (in other words for financial years starting from 1 April 2002). It's these changes that made using a company potentially very attractive.

So how are company profits taxed? There are now three 'official' corporation tax rates:

- Starting Rate   0%
- Small Companies Rate   19%
- Main Rate   30%

Companies with taxable profits of £10,000 or less pay 0%, companies with taxable profits between £50,000 and £300,000 pay 19% and companies with taxable profits exceeding £1,5 million pay 30%.

But what if the profits are between £10,000 and £50,000 or between £300,000 and £1.5 million - what tax rate applies then?

For companies in these "marginal bands" there is a fairly complex formula to calculate the actual tax bill. The starting rate and the small companies rate are withdrawn through a system of so-called 'marginal reliefs'.

Enough of the technical jargon! In fact, we only included the preceding paragraphs in case you've heard of terms like 'starting rate' or 'marginal relief' and want to know what they are.

For practical purposes, when all these strange rates and reliefs are thrown into the mix, corporation tax rates can be simply summarised as follows:

Tax Payable By Companies	
On the first £10,000 profits	0%
On profits between £10,000 and £50,000	23.75%
On profits between £50,000 and £300,000	19%
On profits between £300,000 and £1.5m	32.75%
On profits over £1.5 m	30%

So, for example, a company with profits of £40,000 will pay 0% on the first £10,000 and 23,75% on the remaining £30,000. The total corporation tax bill will be £7,125.

A company with profits of £60,000 would pay 0% on the first £10,000, 23.75% on the next £40,000 and then 19% on the final £10,000. The total corporation tax bill would be £11,400.

Note that £11,400 is simply 19% of £60,000. So to make matters even more simple, it's worth remembering that once profits go over the £50,000 mark, the first two rates can be ignored and profits up to £300,000 are taxed at just 19%.

If your profits are £350,000 you will pay 19% tax on the first £300,000 and 32.75% on the extra £50,000.

Once profits exceed £1.5 million the calculation is also simple - all profits are taxed at a single rate of 30%.

6.3 Changes in the 2004 Budget

However, this is not the end of the matter. In the March 2004 Budget the Chancellor, Gordon Brown, felt that the use of the £10,000 tax free band was being exploited and he changed the rate of corporation tax payable when a company *distributes* its profits as dividends, rather than reinvesting them.

We'll look at dividends shortly, however for the time being all you need to know is that the new provisions will ensure that when a company distributes profits to shareholders, those profits will be subject to corporation tax at a minimum rate of 19%.

The new provisions see the 0% and 23.75% marginal tax rates replaced with the 19% tax rate where profits are passed to shareholders as a dividend after 1 April 2004.

There are a few points to note here:

- It only applies where profits are distributed to shareholders as dividends- if profits are retained within the company, the corporation tax would be calculated as above and the 0% tax band would still be available.

- The effect of a full distribution of profits as a dividend would be to extend the 19% tax band to all taxable profits less than £300,000.

- If you already pay corporation tax at the 19% rate, the new provisions will have no impact on you. As profits of £50,000 or more are already taxed at 19% (or higher) the corporation tax charge will be exactly the same for these companies.

- Where only part of the profits are distributed to shareholders as a dividend, a separate calculation needs to be performed to calculate the corporation tax on the dividends and the corporation tax on the profit retained in the company.

- There are still many benefits to be obtained by incorporating in spite of the hike in the starting rate of corporation tax!

Therefore, in short the new rules will only affect companies with profits of less than £50,000 that distribute profits as dividends.

Let's have a look at a few examples to see how this works based on the current information from the Inland Revenue.

Example

Jack Limited has taxable profits of £20,000. Jack, the sole shareholder does not pay a dividend for the accounting period ended 31 December 2004, preferring to retain the cash within the company for reinvestment. The corporation tax charge would be calculated as:

Taxable profits	£20,000
Less	£10,000
Remaining	£10,000
Corporation tax at 23.75%	£2,375

As no dividend was paid, the 'old' rules apply and the company is still entitled to the £10,000 tax free amount. By contrast, Pete Limited, also has profits of £20,000, but Pete decides to extract the full £20,000 as a dividend.

Pete Limited would pay corporation tax at a rate of 19% on the £20,000 profits as they have all been distributed to the shareholder. Corporation tax of £3,800 would be payable.

An important point to note here is that I have assumed that the company has sufficient cash and profits to account for the corporation tax in addition to the £20,000 dividend.

As the new 19% tax rate applies to profits that have been paid out as a dividend, if the company only had £10,000 profits and cash, the actual dividend payable would not be £10,000, as the company would not then have sufficient cash to pay the £1,900 tax charge. Instead the company would need to pay a dividend of £8,403. The corporation tax charge at 19% on this would be £1,593, and the total dividend and tax would be £10,000, exactly equal to the cash in the company. The new rules have therefore, resulted in an increase in corporation tax of £1,425 – a pretty sizeable increase although, as we'll see later, even taking this into account, using a company is still likely be more tax efficient than being a sole trader.

What about Pete's friend Jake, whose company, Jake Limited makes profits of £100,000 per year. The new dividend tax rules are irrelevant to Jake, as Jake Limited would pay corporation tax of £19,000 anyway whether the profits are extracted or not. I know what your thinking now – what if I want to reinvest some profits and extract the rest. How will this new dividend tax rule affect me? Assuming profits are less than £50,000, you will need to do a special calculation to pro rate the tax rate under the old rules with the new rules. This example will show you how to do it:

Example
Sarah Limited, makes profits of £30,000 per annum. She decides to declare a dividend of £20,000, and retain the remainder within the company.

On the basis of the OLD rules corporation tax would be calculated as follows:
£30,000 – £10,000 x 23.75% = £4,750

The effective tax rate for the £30,000 profits would be £4,750/£30,000= 15.83%.

On the basis of the NEW rules we know that the distributed profits are taxed at 19%:
£20,000 x 19% = £3,800

and the £10,000 remaining is taxed under the OLD rules at 15.83%:

£10,000 x 15.83% = £1,583

The total tax charge will be £5,383 (£3,800 + £1,583).

The interaction of the two rules leads to a small increase in the company's effective tax rate. In this case the total effective tax rate is 17.94% (£5,383/£30,000).

Don't worry about understanding the dividend aspects, we'll cover these later. For the time being all you need to remember is that where a company has profits of less than £50,000, and distributes part of its profits as a dividend, the result will be a mixed tax rate (although still less than the basic rate of income tax!) .

6.4 Associated Companies

Many taxpayers ask whether the main or higher marginal rate of corporation tax can be avoided by simply setting up a whole series of companies each earning less than £300,000.

Wouldn't that be great? Unfortunately, the answer is NO. All of the profit bands and limits described above must be divided up where there are any "associated companies". So what is an associated company?

An associated company is another company under the control of the same persons and their associates. "Associates" has a wide meaning and includes spouses, relatives and business partners.

Therefore, in the most straightforward case, if you form two companies and own all of the shares in both of them, then these companies are associated with each other.

Exceptions:

- A company does not need to be counted as an associated company if it is not carrying on a business.

- Companies that are controlled by relatives other than spouses and minor children do not need to be counted as associated companies unless there is substantial commercial interdependence between the companies.

Subject to the above exceptions, however, <u>any</u> associated company must be taken into account, regardless of in which country it is based or registered and regardless of the kind of business it is carrying on.

Example
Cedric owns 100% of the shares in Fast Cash Ltd (Co. 1), which is making profits of £30,000 in the accounting period ended 30 September 2004.

The corporation tax payable will be £4,750, as the first £10,000 is taxed at 0%, with the remainder taxed at 23.75%.

In order to exploit another gap in the market Cedric sets up Fast Cash UK Limited (Co. 2) in June 2004. If this company simply stays dormant, in other words it does not carry on a trade and has no source of income, it will not be classed as an associated company.

However, if Cedric, starts to invest cash in Co.2 in July 2004 and opens a bank account in August 2004 and starts sending out invoices, Company 2 will be classed as associated with Company 1 for the whole of the accounting period ended 30 September 2004, irrespective of the fact that Co.2 only started to trade in August 2004.

The tax charge for Co.1 will then be £5,700 instead of £4,750. Why? Because the tax bands in the above table are cut in half so that the higher tax rates now kick in at lower profit levels. More precisely, only the first £5,000 is taxed at 0%, the next £20,000 is taxed at 23.75% and the remaining £5,000 is taxed at 19%.

In essence, the two companies have to share the benefit of the lower tax rates.

The general rule is therefore that forming new companies should be carefully reviewed, as this could lead to an unexpected increase in your corporation tax bill.

Hopefully you will now have a clear understanding of the tax rates companies pay. However, the more important question is, how do these rates compare with the tax rates paid by other businesses?

Chapter 7

Corporation Tax versus Income Tax

7.1 Cash Flow Benefits

Unlike a company, which is a separate legal entity, a sole trader business is regarded as an extension of the individual for tax purposes. Therefore all profits generated by the business will be taxed as the income of the individual ("the proprietor").

This is an essential point to grasp. The trader will be taxed on the taxable profits of the business, irrespective of the amounts that are actually taken out of the business as "salary", to pay for living expenses etc.

As a general rule, a sole trader's tax bill has to be settled, along with the submission of the self assessment return, by 31 January following the end of the tax year. A tax year runs from 6 April to the following 5 April. For example, the tax year 2004/2005 will run from 6 April 2004 to 5 April 2005.

In Chapter 5 we briefly outlined the tax pros and cons of using a company. One of the "pros" is that corporation tax is generally paid nine months <u>after</u> the end of the company's accounting period.

In comparison, most sole traders have to make two payments on account – in other words they have to pay their taxes up front. Payments on account are based on the income tax liability of the <u>previous</u> tax year.

The payments on account will be equal amounts based on the actual income tax liability of the preceding year, less any tax already deducted at source.

Example
For the 2004/2005 tax year a sole trader has the following tax bill:

	£
Capital gains tax	10,000
Income tax 35,000	
Tax deducted at source	(20,000)
Net liability	25,000

Payments on account for the 2005/2006 tax year will be as follows:

Income Tax	35,000
Tax deducted at source	(20,000)
	15,000

First payment on account due 31 January 2006   £7,500
Second payment on account due 31 July 2006   £7,500

A balancing payment is also due on 31st January 2007. This will depend on the actual tax liability for 2005/2006 (including any capital gains tax liability), less the payments on account that have already been made.

In conclusion then, many companies enjoy significant cash flow advantages over many sole traders.

7.2 Sole Trader Tax Rates

Sole traders and partners are subject to the same income tax rates as any salary earner or other personal taxpayer. These can be summarised as follows:

Personal Tax Rates 2004/05	
First £4,745	0%
Next £4,746-£6,765	10%
Next £6,576 - £36,145	22%
£36,146 +	40%

So which tax rates are better - the corporation tax ones we outlined above or these personal tax rates? The best way of comparing them is to use some examples.

Let's say Joe Bloggs Limited has taxable profits of £50,000. Put that number into the corporation tax table and you will see that the company's tax bill is only £9,500. But what if Joe Bloggs was a sole trader? Put £50,000 into the income tax table and you will produce a tax bill of £12,208.

Joe has saved £2,708 by trading as a company.

Similarly, a company with profits of £200,000 will pay £38,000 in tax. A sole trader or partner earning the same profits will pay tax of £72,208.

The company pays £34,208 less tax than the sole trader!

Table 1 below compares corporation tax and income tax at other profit levels. This is a worst case scenario and assumes that all profits are distributed to shareholders. This is why when profits are less than £40,000 income tax is actually lower than corporation tax. The £4,745 personal allowance, available to individuals and not companies, significantly lowers the tax charge. At levels above £40,000 the income tax rate jumps up to 40%, and this is where companies really show their mettle. Clearly the difference is enormous and it is these potential tax savings that make trading through a company potentially so attractive.

You should also bear in mind that the corporation tax rates at up to £40,000 assume a full distribution. If you retained income in the company, the rate of corporation tax would be lower - we'll have a look at this in detail a little later on. For now it's worth stating that:

Corporation tax rates can be much lower than income tax rates.

There's something else that is not immediately apparent from a cursory examination of the table. Apart from corporation tax rates being lower than income tax rates at almost every single level of profit, the tax savings become *proportionately* larger as the profits of the business increase.

The reason for this is that companies with profits of between £50,000 and £300,000 pay tax at a flat rate of 19% - the tax rate does not increase as the amount of profit increases. This is fantastic news for business owners. Most tax systems in the Western world are *progressive*, in other words tax rates go up as income/profits go up. But in the UK, a company earning £250,000 pays tax at the same rate as a company earning £50,000. What more incentive do you need to grow your business?

TABLE 1
Corporation Tax vs Income Tax

Profits	Corporation tax	Income tax	Saving
£	£	£	£
10,000	1,900	914	-986
15,000	2,850	2,014	-836
20,000	3,800	3,114	-686
25,000	4,750	4,214	-536
30,000	5,700	5,314	-386
35,000	6,650	6,414	-236
40,000	7,600	8,208	608
50,000	9,500	12,208	2,708
60,000	11,400	16,208	4,808
70,000	13,300	20,208	6,908
80,000	15,200	24,208	9,008
90,000	17,100	28,208	11,108
100,000	19,000	32,208	13,208
120,000	22,800	40,208	17,408
140,000	26,600	48,208	21,608
160,000	30,400	56,208	25,808
180,000	34,200	64,208	30,008
200,000	38,000	72,208	34,208

With personal tax rates, on the other hand, the story is completely different. When your business profits exceed £36,146 every extra pound you earn is taxed at 40%. Not all your profits are taxed at this rate - just amounts in excess of £36,146.

The effect of this is to pull your overall effective tax rate higher and higher as your profits increase. For example, a sole trader earning £50,000 profits only pays tax at an overall rate of 24%; a sole trader earning £200,000 pays tax at 36% because much more of the profit falls into the top tax bracket.

So apart from corporation tax rates being usually lower than personal tax rates the important thing to note is that:

As profits go up, using a company becomes more and more attractive.

Although there are clearly massive differences between the tax burdens facing companies and other unincorporated businesses, so far we have not looked at the complete picture. We've been skewing things in favour of using a company. Why? Because we've ignored the tax position of the *owners* of the company.

For proprietors or partners of unincorporated businesses there is no further tax liability to worry about once income tax has been paid on the profits of the business. However, if a company owner wants to get his hands on the company's profits he has to pay himself a dividend or a salary. This will probably lead to more tax being paid.

The critical question is whether, after paying this extra tax, you're still better off using a company. Answering this very important question, and advising you how to structure your pay, is a major focus of the remainder of this guide. However, before we move on it's important to note that the massive tax savings listed in the above table can, in certain circumstances, be realised in practice and put to good use. To find out how, read on!

7.3 Reinvesting Profits

Although extra tax is payable when profits are withdrawn via a salary or dividend, no extra tax has to be paid if profits are simply *reinvested*. In addition, if profits are less than £50,000, the lower rates of corporation tax will apply. So the next important point to note is that:

Using a company is very attractive if profits are being reinvested.

Why invest profits? One reason would be to grow your company in order to create a valuable business that can be sold at some point in the future. In these circumstances the dividend tax problem does not exist because no dividends are being paid!

Selling your business is probably the most tax-efficient way of making a living in the UK. The proceeds are subject to capital gains tax but if you've owned the company for more than two years, 75% is tax free under the generous taper relief provisions. In effect, selling a business is a way of converting taxable income (future profits, salary, dividends etc) into tax-free capital gains.

Even if you decide not to sell your business, reinvesting profits will result in your earning a higher income in the future, if done wisely. Again using a company will add a great deal more powder to your keg. A company with £50,000 profits has almost £3,000 more to spend on computers or developing new products than a partnership or sole trader. A company with £200,000 profits has almost £35,000 more to invest!

Of course it's very unlikely that all the profits of your business can be reinvested. If you want to pay yourself an income the question as to whether you should incorporate or not becomes a great deal more complex. A whole host of factors come into play: national insurance, how much of the company's profit you would need to extract as dividends, the level of the company's profits and the tax-splitting opportunities available to you and your spouse.

We'll look at each of these factors in starting with national insurance. Before you gulp, there is good news! If you incorporate you may be able to avoid paying national insurance altogether on your income.

Chapter 8

National Insurance Savings

National insurance has become the Government's way of increasing taxes without feeling guilty about breaking election promises. National insurance bills have risen dramatically in recent times.

Some people feel morally obliged to pay national insurance. Strange view. At Taxcafe.co.uk we take the stance that national insurance is just a tax to be avoided like any other.

Before we describe how company owners can avoid paying too much national insurance, it's worth briefly explaining how the tax works.

The key thing to remember is that national insurance is a tax on "earned" income. Your salary is earned income - it rewards your hard work. Dividends, on the other hand, are not earned income - they reward your entrepreneurship. So salaries, bonuses and the like fall into the national insurance net; dividend payments do not.

As a company owner you will be concerned about not just the national insurance you pay on your personal salary but the national insurance the company has to pay as well. That's the problem: companies *and* their employees pay national insurance.

If you incorporate, you and the company are likely to be subject to significantly higher national insurance costs *if you take most of your income as salary*:

- The company will pay class 1 (secondary) national insurance contributions on your salary to the extent that it goes over the lower earnings limit (LEL). The lower earnings limit is currently £4,745. So if your salary is £54,745, the company pays national insurance on £50,000. The company is allowed a tax deduction for the secondary NI that it pays.

- As an employee of the company you will pay class 1 (primary) national insurance on your salary payments made above the £4,745 lower earnings limit.

Up until April 2003 contributions stopped once the upper earning limit was reached. No more. For the 2004/2005 tax year, as a company employee, you will pay class 1 at a rate of 11% between £4,745 and £31,720, and an additional 1% on earnings over £31,720.

Example
John earns a salary of £60,000 per year from his company. His national insurance is calculated as follows.

2002/2003 Tax Year
Employee class 1 primary charge:
£30,420 - £4,615 @ 10% = £2,581

Employer's - class 1 secondary charge:
£60,000 - £4,615 @ 11.8% = £6,589

Total National Insurance £9,170

2004/2005 Tax Year

Employee - class 1 primary charge:
£31,720 - £4,745 @ 11% = £2,967
£60,000 - £31,720 @ 1% = £283

Employer - class 1 secondary charge:
£60,000 - £4,745 @ 12.8% = £7,073

Total National Insurance £10,323

Under this system, John and the company are now paying over £1,000 more tax, even though his income has stayed exactly the same.

How does John's position compare with his friend Dave, who earns exactly the same income and is self employed, in other words has an unincorporated business? Self-employed people have also been hammered by the Chancellor in recent times but they still get away with paying far less national insurance than their peers who are company owners/directors.

A self employed individual is required to pay the following national insurance contributions:

- **Class 2** contributions - these are fixed at £2.05 per week for the 2004/2005 tax year. Annual bill, £107.

- **Class 4** contributions - 8% on profits between the lower and upper profit limits and 1% on profits above the upper profit limit.

So in Dave's case:

£31,720 - £4,745 @ 8% =   £2,158

£60,000 - £31,720 @ 1% =   £283

Class 4 national Insurance   £2,441
Class 2 national insurance   £107
Total national insurance £2,548

There's a massive difference between Dave's and John's national insurance bills.

John pays £7,775 more national insurance than Dave – but they earn the same salary!

Clearly using a company in these circumstances would be a disaster. Dave and John would both pay exactly the same income tax as they both earn the same salary. But because they are subject to different national insurance systems, there's a massive difference in their take-home pays. Dave the sole trader is much better off.

The table below compares the national insurance payable by a sole trader, a 50:50 partnership and a company and its owner (assuming for the company that all profits are extracted as salary).

TABLE 2
National Insurance Bills Compared

Profits	Company	Sole Trader	50:50 Partnership
£	£	£	£
10000	1,251	527	254
20000	3,631	1,327	1,054
30000	6,011	2,127	1,854
40000	7,563	2,345	2,654
50000	8,943	2,448	3,454
60000	10,323	2,548	4,254
70000	11,703	2,648	4,595
80000	13,803	2,748	4,695
90000	14,463	2,848	4,795
100000	15,843	2,948	4,895
110000	17,223	3,048	4,995
120000	18,603	3,148	5,095
130000	19,983	3,248	5,195
140000	21,363	3,348	5,295
150000	22,743	3,448	5,395
160000	24,123	3,548	5,495
180000	26,883	3,748	5,695
200000	29,643	3,948	5,895

At every level of profit the unincorporated businesses are paying less national insurance than the company owner... much less. This leads us to conclude that:

Using a company is a bad idea when all income is taken as salary.

Fortunately there are alternative ways for company owners to pay themselves. We'll now turn to a close examination of the most important one.

Chapter 9

Using Dividends to Escape Tax

One way of avoiding a large national insurance bill is to pay yourself a dividend.

Dividends reward your entrepreneurship, not your work for the company, and are therefore not subject to national insurance. National insurance is a tax on "work" income (salaries, bonuses etc) but not on investment income.

In fact, as we'll see later, dividends can also be used to reduce your income tax.

The important thing to note is that dividends are paid out of profits. If your company doesn't have any profits, it cannot pay any dividends.

Also, because dividends are paid out after all the company's tax calculations have been performed, they are not a tax-deductible expense. Salaries and bonuses are tax deductible, of course. Remember, as a company owner, you are concerned about both your and the company's tax bill. So the fact that the company can claim salaries as a tax deduction, but not dividends, is something that has to be borne in mind when you structure your pay. We'll return to this later.

First of all let's examine how dividends are taxed.

9.1 How Dividends are Taxed

The tax treatment of dividends can be extremely confusing because of terms like "tax credit", "net dividend" and "gross dividend". However, as a general rule:

Higher rate taxpayers pay an effective 25% tax on their dividends.

Other taxpayers pay no tax on their dividends.

If you're interested in the technical details, the taxman treats UK share dividends as having been paid net of tax at 10%. Any dividends paid are grossed up by the fraction 100/90 and are then taxed at either 10% (if the shareholder is a basic rate taxpayer) or 32.5% (if the shareholder is a higher rate taxpayer).

A tax credit equivalent to the amount of the grossing up can then be deducted, although this can never create a repayment of tax.

This is best illustrated by means of a detailed example.

Example
Bob owns a company (Bob Limited) and receives a dividend of £25,000 and no other income. Bob's tax bill for the 2004/05 tax year is calculated as follows:

Bob's tax bill on £25,000 dividend:

	£
Dividend x100/90	27,778
Personal allowance	(4,745)
Taxable income	23,163

Tax:	
£2,020 @ 10%	202
£21,143 @ 10%	2,114
	2,316

Less tax credit	(2,316)

Total tax bill	**NIL**

If Bob received a £60,000 dividend his tax bill would be:

Dividend x100/90	66,667
Personal allowance	(4,745)
Taxable income	61,922

Tax:	
£2,020 @ 10%	202
£29,380 @ 10%	2,938
£30,522 @ 32.5%	9,920
	13,060

Less tax credit	(6,667)

Total tax bill	**6,393**

9.2 Dividends versus Salary

The critical question is, how much better off is Bob by taking a dividend rather than a salary?

Remember with dividends there is only income tax to pay, with salaries there is both income tax and national insurance and national insurance is paid by both Bob and his company.

Let's look at income tax first.

If Bob takes a salary of £25,000, his tax bill for the 2004/05 tax year will be:

	£
Salary	25,000
Less: personal allowance	(4,745)
Taxable income	20,255

Tax:	
£2,020 @10%	202
£18,235 @22%	4,012

Total tax bill   £4,214

By taking dividends instead of salary Bob has saved £4,214 in income tax.

If Bob had taken a salary of £60,000 his tax bill for the 2004/05 tax year would be:

	£
Salary	60,000
Less: personal allowance	(4,745)
Taxable income	55,255

Tax:	
£2,020 @ 10%	202
£29,380 @ 22%	6,464
£23,855 @ 40%	9,542

| **Total tax bill** | **£16,208** |

His tax bill from taking a dividend was only £6,393 compared with £16,208 from taking a salary - a total saving of £9,815.

What about national insurance? Dividends are not subject to national insurance, salary payments are. Both Bob and his company pay national insurance. On a salary of £60,000 national insurance would be payable as follows:

Class 1 primary (paid by Bob)

	£
31,720 - 4,745 x 11%	2,968
28,280 x 1%	283
Total	**3,251**

Class 1 secondary (paid by Bob Limited)

60,000 - 4,745 x 12.8%	**7,073**

Example summary
By taking a dividend, Bob's total tax bill is £6,393. By taking a salary the total tax bill is £16,208 (Bob's income tax) plus £3,251 (Bob's national insurance) plus £7,073 (national insurance paid by Bob Ltd), which comes to a total tax bill of £26,532.

By taking a dividend, Bob has saved £20,139 in tax.

However, before getting too excited it's important to note that we have overlooked one important factor. As we've stated all along, it's important to look at the tax position of both the owner of the company and the company itself.

Companies cannot claim a tax deduction for dividend payments, whereas payments of salary can be claimed. Furthermore, the class 1 secondary national insurance contributions are also tax deductible. The more deductions a company can claim the lower its corporation tax bill.

Impact on the Company's Tax Bill

So taking a dividend may have decreased Bob's tax liability dramatically but it will have increased the company's tax bill. The critical question is whether the increase in the company's tax bill is offset by the drop in Bob's tax bill.

Also bear in mind that this will have a greater impact where a company's profits are less than £50,000, as not only will the dividend not be tax deductible, the rate of corporation tax on those profits extracted will be 19% as the £10,000 tax free band will be withdrawn.

This important issue will be examined shortly. Clearly there are a lot of interrelating factors that have to be taken into account. Before we bring it all together in Chapter 10, let's take a look at some of the other practical factors that may influence the dividend/salary decision.

9.3 Other Important Factors

A number of points must be made about dividends:

Minimum Wage Regulations

It is not possible to extract profits solely by way of dividend. Why? Because as an employee of your company you are likely to come within the National Minimum Wage regulations. Bizarrely, you are not allowed to exploit yourself by paying yourself a very low salary!

That doesn't matter too much because it is usually beneficial to pay yourself a small salary so that you make full use of your £4,745 personal allowance. A salary of £4,745 is tax free and falls below the earnings threshold for national insurance. If your spouse works for the company your family can receive a tax-free salary of £9,490 and pay absolutely no national insurance.

Furthermore, your company will be able to claim the amounts as a tax deduction.

Your Pension

Dividends do not count as "earnings" when it comes to making pension fund contributions. The level of personal pension contributions that you can make is directly linked to your earnings unless you wish to make pension contributions of less than £3,600 pa. Under the stakeholder pension rules, each individual is entitled to make such contributions irrespective of the level of income. For contributions in excess of this, you will require earnings on which the maximum pension is calculated.

Pension contributions attract many tax breaks that you may lose out on if you take too much income in the form of a dividend.

However, the new pension regime allows an individual to elect to either base the earnings figure on the current year or on any year in the preceding four years. Therefore, it is only necessary from a pension-planning perspective, to pay a large salary once every five years.

Personal Service Companies

Certain rules known as "IR35" apply to personal service companies. The effect of the rules is that the company is deemed to pay an amount of salary on 5 April each tax year. The amount of the deemed payment is calculated by the use of a prescribed formula. This negates any benefit from extracting funds by way of a dividend.

A personal service company is a company that employs an individual, and the company is paid for work that the individual does for a third party. Common examples of personal service companies are IT consultants, who establish a company to "collect" payments from customers.

The rules apply where the individual would be an employee of the third party if employed directly by them. The intention of the rules is to catch certain professions (eg IT workers) where an individual operates through a company rather than an unincorporated (sole trader) business. The individuals then pay themselves a dividend rather than a salary to reduce their income tax and national insurance liabilities.

In order for IR35 to apply, the individual must therefore hold a material interest in the company. For this purpose, this is taken to mean more than 5% of the share capital of the company.

Chapter 10

Detailed Examples of Tax Savings

In the previous chapters we've compared corporation tax with income tax, company national insurance with self employment national insurance, and finally the tax treatment of salaries with dividend payments.

Now the time has come to throw all these taxes into the pot and illustrate, with the use of several examples, how much better off you are likely to be by incorporating.

The examples do not take ALL factors into consideration - that could never be achieved. For example, we ignore the potential loss of tax relief on pension contributions. However, they are detailed enough to provide extremely important insights.

The potential tax benefits of using a company depend on:

- The level of taxable profits
- The amount of salary required
- Whether you want to reinvest profits
- Whether a dividend will be paid

The best way to see how these factors interact is to use plenty of examples.

Example 1

Sharon's sole trader business has taxable profits of £14,745, and she usually withdraws all the profits of the business. Her income tax liability is calculated as follows:

	£
Taxable profits	14,745
Less personal allowance	(4,745)
Taxable income	10,000
£2,020 @ 10%	202
£7,980 @ 22%	1,756
National Insurance	
Class 2 (£2.05 p/w x 52)	107
Class 4 (14,745 - 4,745 x 8%)	800

Total tax & national insurance   2,865

If the business is conducted through a company, the tax position will depend on how Sharon withdraws the profits.

If she paid herself a salary of £14,745 the income tax position would be exactly the same as above. Sharon would have a personal tax bill of £1,958 and the salary would be tax deductible, bringing the company's taxable profits to zero.

The national insurance position would clearly change. Sharon would pay class 1 primary contributions of £1,100 (£14,745 - £4,745 @ 11%) and the company would pay class 1 secondary contributions of £1,280 (£14,745 - £4,745 @ 12.8%), although a tax deduction would be given for the class 1 secondary contributions paid. She only pays £907 national insurance as a sole trader.

As an alternative, she could pay herself a salary of £4,745 (to use up her personal income tax allowance) and a dividend of the remaining £10,000. The combined (Sharon and her company) tax position can be summarised as follows:

Company's tax position

	£
Taxable profits (£14,745 - £4,745)	10,000
Corporation tax 19/119	1,597

Sharon's tax position

Salary	4,745
Personal allowance	(4,745)
Dividend	8,403
Gross dividend: £10,000 x100/90	9,337
Tax @ 10%	934
Less tax credit	(934)
Tax payable	NIL

No national insurance contributions are payable as dividends are exempt from national insurance and the salary is below the lower earnings limit.

Total tax saving using a company: £1,268 on business profits of £14,745.

Example 2
Let's now assess the effect of the above strategy (taking a low salary, with the remaining cash extracted via a dividend) where the taxable profits are significantly higher.

Rohan's business generates a profit of £60,000 for the 2004/2005 tax year.

If he remained as a sole trader, his total income tax and national insurance would be as follows:

Income tax:	£
Profits	60,000
Personal allowance	(4,745)
Taxable income	55,255
£2,020 @ 10%	202
£31,400 – £2,020 @ 22%	6,463.6
£23,855 @ 40%	9,542
Total income tax	16,207.6

National Insurance:	
Class 2 NIC	107
Class 4 NIC	2,441
Total tax & NI	**18,756**

If the trade was conducted through a company, and Rohan withdrew a salary of £4,745 with the remainder as dividends, the position would be:

	£
Business profits	60,000
Salary	(4,745)
Company profit	55,255
Corporation tax	(10,498)
Available for dividend	44,757
Higher rate tax	5,957
Lower rate tax	3,140
Tax credit	(4,985)
Total taxes	**14,610**

A saving of over £4,000 tax and national insurance.

Table 3 below compares the total tax bill at numerous other profit levels for a sole trader, company and partnership taking into account income tax, national insurance, corporation tax, and the tax deductibility of salaries and employer's class 1 national insurance.

The following assumptions are used:

- There are no associated companies.
- As regards the company, a small salary is paid equivalent to the personal allowance, with the remainder of the profits withdrawn by way of dividend to the sole shareholder.
- The sole trader has no employees.
- The partnership is a 50:50 partnership.

TABLE 3
Total Tax Bills Compared

Profits	Sole Trader	Partnership	Company
10,000	1,441	305	839
20,000	4,441	2,881	2,616
30,000	7,441	5,881	4,584
40,000	10,555	8,881	6,675
50,000	14,655	11,881	10,666
60,000	18,755	14,881	14,622
70,000	22,855	17,422	18,548
80,000	26,955	21,110	22,473
90,000	31,055	25,210	26,398
100,000	35,155	29,310	30,323
110,000	39,255	33,410	34,248
120,000	43,355	37,510	38,173
130,000	47,455	41,610	42,098
140,000	51,555	45,710	46,023
150,000	55,655	49,810	49,948
160,000	59,755	53,910	53,873
170,000	63,855	58,010	57,798
180,000	67,955	62,110	61,723
190,000	72,055	66,210	65,648
200,000	76,155	70,310	69,573
210,000	80,255	74,410	73,498
220,000	84,355	78,510	77,423
230,000	88,455	82,610	81,348
240,000	92,555	86,710	85,273
250,000	96,655	90,810	89,198
260,000	100,755	94,910	93,123
270,000	104,855	99,010	97,048
280,000	108,955	103,110	100,973
290,000	113,055	107,210	104,898

TABLE 3
Total Tax Bills Compared (contd)

Profits	Sole Trader	Partnership	Company
300,000	117,155	111,310	108,823
310,000	121,255	115,410	112,748
320,000	125,355	119,510	116,673
330,000	129,455	123,610	120,598
340,000	133,555	127,710	128,158
350,000	137,655	131,810	133,115
400,000	158,155	152,310	157,896
450,000	178,655	172,810	182,677
500,000	199,155	193,310	207,458
550,000	219,655	213,810	232,240
600,000	240,155	234,810	257,021
650,000	260,655	254,810	281,802
700,000	281,155	275,310	306,583
750,000	301,655	295,810	331,365
800,000	322,155	316,310	356,146
850,000	342,655	336,810	380,927
900,000	363,155	357,310	405,708
950,000	383,655	377,810	430,490
1,000,000	404,155	398,310	455,271
1,050,000	424,655	419,810	480,052
1,100,000	445,155	439,310	504,833
1,150,000	465,655	459,810	529,615
1,200,000	486,155	480,310	554,396
1,250,000	506,655	500,810	579,177
1,300,000	527,155	521,310	603,958
1,350,000	547,655	541,810	628,740
1,400,000	568,155	562,310	653,521
1,450,000	588,655	582,810	678,302
1,500,000	609,155	603,310	703,083

To understand the table better, let's take a sample profit figure, eg £100,000, and compare how the above numbers were calculated.

a) Sole trader

Income tax:	£
£100,000 - £4,745	95,255
£2,020 @ 10%	202
£31,400 - £2,020 @ 22%	6,464
£95,255 - £31,400 @ 40%	25,542
Total	32,208

National insurance	
Class 4:	
£31,720 - £4,745 @ 8%	2,157
£100,000 - £31,720 @ 1%	683
Class 2	107
Total	2,947

Total income tax & national insurance: £35,155.

b) Partnership

Each partner assessed on £50,000 profits.

Income tax:	£
£50,000 - £4,745	45,255
£2,020 @10%	202
£31,400 - £2,020 @ 22%	6,464
£45,255 - £31,400 @ 40%	5,542
Total	12,208

National insurance:
Class 4:

£31,720 - £4,745 @ 8%	2,157
£50,000 - £31,720 @ 1%	183
Class 2	107
Total	2,447

Total income tax and national insurance for each partner: £14,655.

For the partnership, total tax and national insurance is £29,310.

c) Company

Corporation tax:
The director's salary of £4,745 is not subject to income tax or national insurance, as it equals the tax-free personal allowance and is below the lower earnings limit.

	£
Taxable profits of company:	
£100,000 - £4,745	95,255
Corporation tax £95,255 @ 19%	18,098

Income tax on dividends:

Amount available for dividend:	
£95,255 - £18,098	77,157
Grossed up:	
£77,157 x 100/90	85,730
£31,400 @ 10%	3,140
£54,330 @ 32.5%	17,658
Less tax credit	(8,573)
Income tax	12,224

Total tax and national insurance £30,323

Summary

Looking at the above table we can see that based on the assumptions stated above, the company route would result in lower overall tax for profit levels up to between £400,000 and £450,000.

The reason why the company loses its attractiveness in purely tax terms at higher profit levels is that the corporation tax payable by the company is at a rate of 32.75%. This is substantially above the 19%-23.75% rates payable at lower profit levels.

Note that when comparing the partnership with the company, a fairer comparison would be to have *two* directors/shareholders drawing a salary and taking dividends.

This would result in an even lower tax charge for the company due to the availability of two personal allowances and two basic-rate tax bands for dividend payments.

The tax payable, assuming two directors drawing a salary equal to the personal allowance, and taking the remainder of profits as dividends, is summarised in Table 4 below. We've also included the partnership tax from Table 3 as a comparison.

TABLE 4
Partnership vs Two-director Company

Taxable profits	Partnership	Company
£	£	£
10,000	305	81
20,000	2,881	1,695
30,000	5,881	3,648
40,000	8,881	5,625
50,000	11,881	7,611
60,000	14,881	9,597
70,000	17,422	11,497
80,000	21,110	13,545
90,000	25,210	17,470
100,000	29,310	21,395
110,000	33,410	25,320
120,000	37,510	29,245
130,000	41,610	33,170
140,000	45,710	37,095
150,000	49,810	41,020

You may be wondering about the effect of paying a substantial salary, as opposed to dividends. The answer is that at the higher profit levels there is not much difference between salary or dividend payments.

This is because, although dividends are subject to lower income tax in the hands of the shareholder, salary payments are tax deductible.

At profit levels above £300,000 the deduction is worth £3,275 for every £10,000 paid out. (This is because the company's corporation tax rate is 32,75% so every £10,000 paid out in salaries is £10,000 that escapes corporation tax.)

Example

Suppose, Cedric Ltd is making taxable profits of £400,000 per annum. Cedric decides to pay himself a salary of £350,000, with the remainder as dividends.

Corporation tax:	£
Taxable profits	400,000
Less: salary	(350,000)
Less employer's NI	(44,193)
Profits	5,807
Corporation tax @ 19%	1,103

Income tax:	
Salary	350,000
Income tax	132,208
Net Dividend	4,704
Income tax	1,176
National insurance	6,150

Total tax and national insurance: £145,341.

This compares with £157,896 from Table 3 when most of the income was taken as a dividend. There are therefore some useful savings to be gained by adjusting the dividend/salary mix.

Overall, it is likely to almost always be beneficial from a tax standpoint to pay dividends where the company's taxable profits are less than £300,000.

For profit levels above this, the tax-deductible nature of the salary payments erodes the tax benefits of dividends, and a full calculation taking into account the shareholder's effective rate of tax should be undertaken.

You have to assess which carries the most "weight": the lower income tax on dividends versus the tax deductibility of the salary.

Furthermore, when the tax savings are marginal you also have to take other factors into consideration. For example, a salary may be more attractive if you want to be able to make contributions into a pension fund.

Finally, in the above examples we have made one very important assumption: all of the profits are taken out of the business. But what if a significant percentage is retained to fund future growth of the business?

This is where companies really show their mettle.

Chapter 11

Reinvesting Profits to Make Big Tax Savings

Of course, not all shareholders wish to extract all of the available profits from the company on an annual basis. In fact this is one of the key advantages of the company, in that it gives you a choice as to whether you wish to withdraw the profits or not. If you choose to leave funds within the business to fund future growth, only corporation tax will be paid on the profits retained within the company, and this will also potentially reduce the company's rate of corporation tax. If the taxable profits are less than £50,000 the 19% dividend tax rate would only be used for the proportion of the profits distributed as a dividend.

By contrast, with a sole trader/partnership, the proprietors of the business are taxed on the annual taxable profits irrespective of whether they are retained within the business or taken by the proprietor as drawings.

Clearly, retaining profits within the company will significantly reduce the overall tax liability.

The table below compares the tax liability of a sole trader and a 50:50 partnership with a company at different profit levels. The difference here from Table 3 above, is that whilst the shareholder is paying himself a salary equivalent to the personal allowance, he is extracting only 50% of the profits by way of dividend. The remaining 50% is retained within the company to fund growth of the business and cover the corporation tax liability.

Again, if the company had two shareholders (to give a fairer comparison with a 50:50 partnership), the total tax payable by the company would be even lower!

The table speaks for itself: when a business is reinvesting and using retained earnings as a source of finance, incorporation has significant advantages.

Given that most small companies will be seeking to reinvest at least some of their profits, this is where the key tax benefit arises.

Most of the examples above are based on the shareholder/employee taking a salary equal to the personal allowance, with the remainder as dividends. The decision as to whether a salary or bonus is required can be complex and would usually need to be taken on an annual basis. The following points need to be borne in mind:

- Dividends are taxed at effective rates of 0% and 25%, as opposed to 10%, 22% and 40% for a bonus/salary.

- Salary payments fall into the PAYE regime, whereas tax on a dividend is paid by 31 January following the end of the tax year.

- Dividends are not subject to national insurance.

- The company cannot claim a tax deduction for dividend payments.

TABLE 5
Total Tax Bills Compared
50% Profit Reinvested

Profits £	Sole Trader £	Partnership £	Company £
10,000	1,441	305	798
20,000	4,441	2,881	2,330
30,000	7,441	5,881	4,321
40,000	10,555	8,881	6,395
50,000	14,655	11,881	8,498
60,000	18,755	14,881	10,933
70,000	22,855	17,422	14,083
80,000	26,955	21,110	17,233
90,000	31,055	25,210	20,383
100,000	35,155	29,310	23,533
110,000	39,255	33,410	26,683
120,000	43,355	37,510	29,833
130,000	47,455	41,610	32,983
140,000	51,555	45,710	36,133
150,000	55,655	49,810	39,283
160,000	59,755	53,910	42,433
170,000	63,855	58,010	45,583
180,000	67,955	62,110	48,733
190,000	72,055	66,210	51,883
200,000	76,155	70,310	55,033
210,000	80,255	74,410	58,183
220,000	84,355	78,510	61,333
230,000	88,455	82,610	64,483
240,000	92,555	86,710	67,633
250,000	96,655	90,810	70,783
260,000	100,755	94,910	73,933
270,000	104,855	99,010	77,083
280,000	108,955	103,110	80,233
290,000	113,055	107,210	83,383
300,000	117,155	111,310	86,533

TABLE 5
Total Tax Bills Compared
50% Profit Reinvested (Contd)

Profits £	Sole Trader £	Partnership £	Company £
310,000	121,255	115,410	90,406
320,000	125,355	119,510	94,931
330,000	129,455	123,610	99,456
340,000	133,555	127,710	103,981
350,000	137,655	131,810	108,506
400,000	158,155	152,310	131,131
450,000	178,655	172,810	153,756
500,000	199,155	193,310	176,381
550,000	219,655	213,810	199,006
600,000	240,155	234,810	221,631
650,000	260,655	254,810	244,256
700,000	281,155	275,310	266,881
750,000	301,655	295,810	289,506
800,000	322,155	316,310	312,131
850,000	342,655	336,810	334,756
900,000	363,155	357,310	357,381
950,000	383,655	377,810	380,006
1,000,000	404,155	398,310	402,631
1,050,000	424,655	419,810	425,256
1,100,000	445,155	439,310	447,881
1,150,000	465,655	459,810	470,506
1,200,000	486,155	480,310	493,131
1,250,000	506,655	500,810	515,756
1,300,000	527,155	521,310	538,381
1,350,000	547,655	541,810	561,006
1,400,000	568,155	562,310	583,631
1,450,000	588,655	582,810	606,256
1,500,000	609,155	603,310	628,881

However, comparing a one shareholder company with a partnership is not really a true comparison. The table below shows the total tax payable assuming a two person company with both shareholders extracting 50% of the gross profits by way of a dividend.

TABLE 6
Total Tax Bills Compared:
1 versus 2 Directors/Shareholders
50% Profit Reinvested

Profits	1 Person	2 Persons
£	£	£
10,000	798	0
20,000	2,330	1,906
30,000	4,321	3,521
40,000	6,395	5,478
50,000	8,498	7,525
60,000	10,933	9,597
70,000	14,083	11,497
80,000	17,233	13,397
90,000	20,383	15,297
100,000	23,533	17,197
110,000	26,683	19,097
120,000	29,833	20,997
130,000	32,983	22,897
140,000	36,133	25,083
150,000	39,283	28,233

This shows more clearly that there are opportunities to minimise the overall tax charge particularly where significant reinvestment of profits is expected.

As shown in Table 5, a partnership with profits of £150,000 would pay £49,810 in tax, whereas a two person company reinvesting 50% of profits would only pay £28,233 in tax.

When you add on the opportunity to extract cash tax free via a loan account (see below) and the potential benefits of using an offshore company structure (see Chapter 16), incorporation still looks extremely attractive to many businesses!

Chapter 12

How to Pay Dividends

One issue that needs to be addressed is the financial requirements of the shareholder/employee. Given that a low salary is paid in most of the above examples, as a matter of cash flow it may be that the employee requires more cash per month to be extracted than the low salary will allow. In this circumstance, one question is: how often can a dividend be paid?

In theory, there is nothing to prevent dividends being paid weekly. However, this would be scrutinised by the Inland Revenue which may contend that the payments are in fact salary and therefore PAYE and national insurance would be applicable. It is for this reason that a director's loan account is often used.

12.1 Directors' Loan Accounts

A loan account is used by employees, usually controlling directors, to withdraw cash from the company. A dividend is then paid to clear the loan account, at a given time.

The advantage of this is that it eliminates the need to pay monthly dividends. Instead a dividend can be paid every, say, three months to clear the account.

There are a few issues that need to be borne in mind when considering the use of loan accounts:

- A benefit in kind arises in the director's hands if an interest-free/or low-interest loan is granted and exceeds £5,000.

  The benefit in kind is calculated as the difference between the interest charge actually levied and the interest charge that should have been levied using the Inland Revenue's 'standard' interest rate (known as the 'official rate of interest').

  The benefit is included with the employee's salary and subject to income tax.

- If the loan is still outstanding nine months and one day after the company's year end, a tax charge equivalent to 25% of the amount of the loan must be paid to the Inland Revenue. This tax charge is repayable if the loan is repaid.

- If the loan account is cleared with a salary or bonus payment, the taxman will treat the amount of the loan as being subject to PAYE.

Example
Jack and his wife own the entire share capital of their company, Hill Limited. They need to withdraw profits regularly to fund their living expenses but would rather not pay salary, due to the national insurance consequences etc.

They could certainly pay themselves a small salary with very little tax impact. For example, a salary of £5,000 per year each could be paid at a cost to each of them, in terms of tax and national insurance, of approximately £80. The company would then obtain a tax deduction for the £10,000 salaries, along with the associated employer's national insurance (approximately £100).

They could then withdraw cash as directors up to the £5,000 limit, before clearing this with a dividend payment.

Therefore they could each extract further cash of £1,000 per month for four months, before paying a dividend to clear the remaining balance. If possible, the actual cash should actually be paid to the directors, as opposed to a simple bookkeeping entry reducing the loan account and reflecting a dividend payment.

One key factor to bear in mind here is that in order for a dividend payment to be made, the company must have sufficient distributable profits.

Distributable profits are, broadly speaking, accumulated profits less losses. Therefore if a company has made losses of £100,000 in the period since incorporation, yet makes a profit of £50,000, it does not yet have any distributable profits, as the company is showing an accumulated loss of £50,000.

12.2 How to Make a Dividend Payment

It is important when making a payment to employees/directors that it is correctly classed as salary or dividend. This may seem fairly obvious but there are a number of factors that the Inland Revenue will look at to determine whether a payment is in fact salary.

In general terms it is for the directors and shareholders of a company to determine the amount of a dividend and therefore, provided all proper procedures have been followed, any attempt by the taxman to argue that a payment should be reclassified as salary would be unlikely to be successful on general principles.

Note that in the examples above, a salary has been used equivalent to the personal allowance. Whilst there is nothing actually wrong with paying such a salary (as this will ensure no national insurance is payable), many small businesses prefer to pay a rounded payment such as £5,000 in salary and account for some PAYE and national insurance.

The tax anti-avoidance provisions that Inland Revenue has at its disposal are fairly specific and are in the most part cumbersome to apply. Simply paying a salary equivalent to the personal allowance would be unlikely to fall foul of these, provided proper procedures are followed. The only current risk in paying a non-commercially low salary is that Inland Revenue has used this as one of the factors in assessing whether the settlement provisions should be used.

The settlement provisions allow the taxman to argue that, by paying a low salary and the remainder in dividends to two or more shareholders, the dividends should be taxed solely on the main 'working' shareholder

In addition, in order to obtain a tax deduction for any salary payments, it would need to be shown to be made wholly and exclusively for the purposes of the trade of the company. The taxman could therefore certainly challenge a salary paid to a non-working spouse who had little input into the running of the business.

It is therefore sensible to keep records of the work undertaken in exchange for the salary payments or other evidence showing the cost if the services of a third party are to be obtained.

There are a number of formalities that should be observed when making dividend and salary payments to ensure that the legal procedures are followed.

The question of whether a dividend is unlawful or not is not primarily an issue for the Inland Revenue. Instead it is determined by the company's articles of association and the Companies Act. The articles of association ('articles') are essentially the internal rules of the company and will determine how the company is run. It is possible to have custom articles drafted by a lawyer but, in most cases, the company formation agent will simply use a standard template.

Every company has to have a company secretary, so it would normally fall to them to consider the legality of dividend payments.

If the correct procedures are not followed, the Inland Revenue can argue that a dividend payment has not been lawfully made. They could then class the payments as salary, and subject them to PAYE and national insurance or more likely, illegal dividends could be classed as a loan to directors, with the possibility of both a company and personal tax charge (see 12.1).

The first point to note is that generally the shareholders must agree to a dividend payment, although for interim dividends (in other words payments during the accounting period) the directors may authorise payment, without the shareholders' consent at a general meeting.

In most cases this will not be a big issue if the shareholders are also the directors!

The following formalities should be observed when making dividend payments:

- Minutes of directors' meetings authorising the dividend should be drafted and dated.

- Dividend vouchers showing the net and gross dividend paid per share, along with the total amount paid should be issued by the company secretary to the shareholders.

- You should retain any evidence (forecasts etc) you have available to support your view that there would be sufficient distributable profits to make a dividend payment. If there is any doubt as to whether there will be sufficient distributable profits you should draw up interim accounts to determine the level of distributable profits.

- The dividend payments should be correctly recorded in the company's accounting records.

12.3 Illegal Dividends

There is a big difference between the treatment of legal and illegal dividends. Legal dividends are dividends that are made out of company profits with the correct payment procedures being followed.

Illegal dividends would usually be made where the company does not have sufficient retained profits to cover the dividend payments. In this case, the excess would be classed as illegal. That is why it is important to ensure that the company has enough profits (note profits, not cash!). If there is any doubt, draft accounts should be drawn up.

Section 277 of the Companies Act 1985 states that a shareholder who knows or has reasonable grounds to believe that a dividend or part of it is unlawful is liable to repay it or that part of it to the company.

There is an exception if the shareholder is innocent and doesn't know the dividend is illegal, although this will only really apply to larger quoted companies. In most small private companies, particularly where the directors are also the controlling shareholders, the Inland Revenue would assume that the shareholders would know the status of the dividend.

Where this applies the company is not classed as distributing income to the shareholder, and the shareholder holds the cash as a trustee for the company. In essence for most small private companies, this will mean that it will be treated as a loan to the shareholder and the associated tax implications as stated in 12.1 would follow. This is potentially costly in tax terms, as the company could be landed with a 25% tax charge on the amount of the loan, and the shareholder/director could be taxed on a market interest rate as a benefit in kind.

Chapter 13

Using Your Spouse For Further Tax Savings

It is frequently advised that a business should make full use of the tax-free/low-tax bands of the spouses.

There are two distinct issues:

- Whether to employ the other spouse and pay him or her a salary, with the company claiming this payment as a tax deduction.

- Whether both spouses should subscribe for shares in the company on incorporation and then pay themselves dividends.

If we compare a company with one director/shareholder taking a salary equivalent to the personal allowance, and withdrawing the remainder by way of dividends, with a company with two directors/shareholders following the same strategy, we can see that two personal allowances/basic-rate bands can lead to some useful tax savings:

TABLE 7
Total Tax Bills Compared:
1 versus 2 Directors/Shareholders

Profits	1 Person	2 Persons
£	£	£
10,000	998	97
20,000	2,898	1,997
30,000	4,798	3,897
40,000	6,773	5,797
50,000	10,698	7,697
60,000	14,623	9,597
70,000	18,548	11,497
80,000	22,473	13,545
90,000	26,398	17,470
100,000	30,323	21,395
110,000	34,248	25,320
120,000	38,173	29,245
130,000	42,098	33,170
140,000	46,023	37,095
150,000	49,948	41,020

In the past twelve months, the Inland Revenue has become increasingly interested in husband and wife companies and in some cases they have challenged techniques similar to those outlined above and demanded significant tax payments (sometimes £40,000 to £50,000 in back taxes).

13.1 What is the Taxman's Thinking?

The Inland Revenue is using part of the "settlements legislation" to effectively challenge the income assessable on non-working spouses.

The settlement provisions provide that where a person makes a settlement (which includes making a gift of an asset), any income arising from the property will be taxed in the hands of the person making the settlement, if the income could become payable to him or to his spouse. For the legislation to apply, there has to be an element of "bounty" - something given to the other party in exchange for no consideration.

However, there is a special exemption which excludes from these provisions an outright gift by one spouse to the other *unless* the property gifted is "wholly or substantially a right to income".

Up until recently, the taxman has not interpreted this as applying to husband and wife companies and it has always been assumed that any gift of shares in a small company is not just a "right to income" but in reality is much more.

The Inland Revenue is applying the settlements legislation very widely, although as relates to husband and wife companies, they are targeting two key situations:

- Husband/wife companies where both parties subscribe for shares on incorporation.

- Husband/wife companies where one spouse subscribes for shares on incorporation and subsequently gifts some of the shares to the other spouse.

Both of these scenarios are very common, and the effect of the settlements legislation applying would be that dividends received by the basic-rate taxpayer are assessed on the other spouse, frequently a higher-rate taxpayer.

For both situations the taxman will look for the company having a low capital base, with the majority of the work undertaken by just one of the spouses.

The low capital value of the company indicates to the taxman that the shares do not represent ownership rights over a large amount of assets but are, in effect, a right to income from the company.

Inland Revenue has published a tax bulletin outlining its interpretation of the law. This is useful and contains a number of examples (see below) that explain the taxman's thinking.

It should be noted that many tax advisers are confident that Inland Revenue's application of the settlements legislation to husband and wife companies is incorrect.

13.2 Where the Settlements Provisions Apply

Subscribed Shares

E Ltd was incorporated in October 1997 to provide the services of Mr E as an IT consultant to a number of clients working in the pharmaceuticals industry. The company's share capital is £2 consisting of two £1 shares. Mr E is the sole director of the company and his wife Mrs E is company secretary but takes no other active part in the company. From the beginning each subscribed for one share. The company has no significant capital assets. The figures for the first year's trading are:

	£
Turnover	100,000
Expenses	(5,000)
Salary, Mr E	(10,000)
Salary, Mrs E	(5,000)
Dividends	(70,000)

In this case, Mrs E receives a salary for her duties as company secretary, but the whole arrangement whereby Mrs E invests £1 and in return gets a dividend of £35,000 is 'bounteous'. There is nothing to suggest that the dividend is a commercial return on her investment. As there is no significant capital in the company, what has passed from Mr E to Mrs E is substantially a right to income and the whole of the dividend is taxed in Mr E's hands.

In reaching this conclusion, the legislation allows Inland Revenue to look at the whole arrangement. It is the work that Mr E carries out which creates the company's profits, which in turn enables the dividends to be paid. Mrs E's investment of £1 does not enable the company to make profits and the company itself has minimal capital value. In accepting a salary below the market rate from the company, and thereby allowing some of the income earned to pass to Mrs E as a dividend, Mr E has entered into a bounteous arrangement to divert income to his spouse with the aim of avoiding tax.

Subscribed Shares with Little Capital Value

As above, but in October 1997 Mr E was not married and subscribed for both £1 shares himself. Mr E's solicitor was acting as company secretary. A year later he married and gave his wife one of his shares in the company. At this point Mrs E took over the role of company secretary. In the following year Mrs E receives a wage of £5,000 and the company pays a dividend of £35,000 per share.

Since the capital value of the company is insignificant, the gift of the share from Mr E to his wife is "wholly or substantially a right to income". Accordingly the settlements legislation applies in relation to Mrs E's £35,000 dividend payment and the income would be treated as Mr E's for tax purposes.

13.3 Where Settlement Provisions Don't Apply

An Outright Gift to a Spouse

Mrs L owns 10,000 ordinary shares in a FTSE 100 company. Those shares are worth £40,000. Mrs L gives those shares to her husband. Mr L is now entitled to all the dividends from the shares and can sell the shares if he wishes to keep the proceeds. This is an outright gift of shares that are not wholly, or substantially, a right to income since they have a capital value and can be traded, so the settlements legislation does not apply.

Subscribed Shares

Mr M is the sole director and owns all the 100 ordinary shares in M Limited, a small manufacturing company. The company employs 10 people and owns a small factory, a high street shop, tools fixtures and fittings and three delivery vehicles. Mr M draws a salary of £30,000 each year and receives dividends of £20,000. Mr M then gifts 50 shares to his wife who plays no part in the business. Mr and Mrs M then each receive dividends of £10,000.

The taxman would not seek to apply the settlements legislation to the dividends received by Mrs M. This is because the outright gift of the shares cannot be regarded as wholly or substantially a right to income. The shares have capital rights and the company has substantial assets, so on the winding up or sale of the business the shares would have more than an insubstantial value.

Let's take a look at another example. Mr N wants to set up in business as a bookseller. He needs at least £100,000 to buy premises, equipment and stock. He sets up a company and he and Mrs N each subscribe for 40,000 ordinary £1 shares at par value and the company borrows £20,000 from the bank. Mr N draws a salary, which after four years is £40,000. Mrs N does not work for the company. Company profits are used to repay debt and expand the business. The business does well and after six years the profits are sufficient to pay a dividend of £10,000.

The taxman would not seek to apply the settlements legislation to the dividend of £5,000 received by Mrs N. There is no bounty as Mr N draws a commercial salary for his efforts and the dividend is a commercial return on the initial investment which was vital at the commencement of the business and contained a clear element of risk.

It is worthwhile having a sense of perspective about this. The Inland Revenue has stated that they have no plans to significantly increase the number of formal enquiries they undertake in this area.

There has not yet been a definitive hearing before the courts and even if Inland Revenue was to argue that the settlement legislation applied, it is clear that they will take account of commercial reasons for the arrangement.

The extract below is an extract from an actual Inland Revenue letter:

"The provisions in s660A apply to deem the dividends received by Mrs X to be her husband's income for all Income Tax purposes. As he is liable to tax at the higher rates some additional liability will arise.

I realise that Mrs X performed her duties for the company without remuneration. I can therefore accept that part of the dividend she received represents a reasonable reward for her services. Given the hours she worked I have taken this part to be equal to 50% of the dividends paid in the accounting period."

It therefore seems that you should ensure that you retain evidence showing the extent of duties provided by both husband and wife shareholders as this could be useful in justifying the income splitting nature of dividends.

13.4 Joint Assets

One of the little known changes made in the 2004 Budget was to change the income tax treatment of certain jointly held assets.

Previously, income from assets such as shares jointly held by a husband and wife was automatically taxed 50:50, irrespective of the actual beneficial ownership of the shares. One spouse was allowed to own the majority of the shares but income tax savings were achieved by dividing the dividends equally. If required, an election was allowed to be made to have income taxed according to the actual beneficial entitlements.

This loophole was being used to circumvent the settlement provisions.

Under the new rules, the 50:50 basis will no longer apply, and the dividends from shares in close companies (which will in practice include practically all small owner managed companies) will be taxed according to the actual interests.

13.5 Summary

The Inland Revenue's policy, if accepted by the courts, would therefore have a major impact on the incorporation of sole trade husband and wife businesses where:

- The capital value of the company is low.

- One spouse does the majority of work in the company.

- Cash is extracted predominantly by dividends and an "uncommercially low" salary is paid.

These rules should not prevent individuals transferring shares to their spouses, if that is what they wish to do, as such a transfer is a legitimate tax planning exercise. Each case will be looked at on its merits.

In particular, the Inland Revenue's policy on the use of the settlement rules is contrary to the freedom married couples have to transfer assets free of capital gains tax and inheritance tax.

The arguments to be put before the courts vary from rejecting the "substantially a right to income" argument, to suggesting that in many divorce proceedings the spouse would probably be entitled to 50% of the other spouse's assets in any case.

It should be noted that the settlement provisions attack the effective doubling of the tax-free dividend band for husband and wife companies and do not attack the payment of dividends to working spouses.

13.6 Dividend Waivers

We are sometimes asked whether all shareholders need to receive a dividend, or whether you can 'pick and choose' the receiving shareholders.

This would clearly be a significant bonus if you could, as you would be able to channel profits to the shareholders with the lowest income for a particular tax year.

However, this is not the case. Dividends are payable in direct proportion to your shareholdings, therefore a 33% shareholder would in general be entitled to 33% of the declared dividend. There are, however, other options available.

Firstly, different classes of share capital could be used, for example A and B shares. The dividend declared for A shares could be different to the B shares, or alternatively preference shares could be used, giving the shareholder a fixed dividend/return on their investment, yet allowing this to be still taxed as a dividend receipt.

The Inland Revenue can and has applied the settlement legislation to preference shares used to split income, as arguably they represent little more than a right to income. (At least with ordinary shares there is the argument that the shares represent a lot more than just dividend receipts, in that they relate to underlying ownership of the assets of the company.)

Secondly, a shareholder could waive the right to receive dividends. The risk here is that Inland Revenue could apply the settlement provisions. The taxman can argue that the person making the waiver has indirectly provided funds to another and that the settlements legislation is in point.

Much would depend on the facts of the dividend waiver, however the Inland Revenue would look out for the following factors, which would indicate that the settlements legislation is likely to apply:

- The level of retained profits, is not enough to allow the same rate of dividend to be paid to all shareholders.
- Although there are sufficient retained profits to pay the same rate of dividend per share for the year in question, there has been a history of waivers over several years where the total dividends payable in the absence of the waivers exceed profits.
- There is any other evidence, which suggests that the same rate would not have been paid to all shareholders in the absence of the waiver.
- The non-waiving shareholders are persons whom the waiving shareholder can reasonably be regarded as wishing to benefit by the waiver.
- The non-waiving shareholder would pay less tax on the dividend than the waiving shareholder

In addition, a dividend waiver could be a potentially exempt transfer ('PET') for inheritance tax purposes, and as such the amount of the waiver would be classed as part of the giftor's estate unless they survived for at least 7 years from the date of the gift.

If you're contemplating a dividend waiver you need to carefully consider whether it could be questioned by the Inland Revenue, in particular, it is essential that there are sufficient profits to distribute the chosen dividend to all shareholders if desired.

13.7 Retaining Cash within the Company

One point that is sometimes raised is whether cash can be retained within the company and subsequently extracted a number of years later. This may be due to cash flow issues or potential offshore opportunities (see Chapter 16).

In general there will be few significant issues with this. If money was left on loan account, the company could be charged interest by the shareholder (at a market rate). This would be allowed as a tax deductible expense for the company and would be taxed as interest income in the shareholder's hands.

This would be taxed before dividends and could potentially have the effect of pushing more of the dividends into the higher rate tax band.

The cash retained in the company would already have suffered a corporation tax charge. The only impact would be if the cash balances were significant.

In order to qualify as a business asset for both capital gains tax and inheritance tax, and thereby gain the beneficial reliefs (business asset taper relief and business property relief) the company must be a trading company.

When assessing whether a company is a trading company the Inland Revenue will look at a variety of issues, including the annual accounts.

The taxman has stated that if there are significant non trading assets, this could impair the trading status of the company, with the result that business asset taper relief and business property relief could be restricted.

One of the examples they list as non trading assets would be substantial cash retained in the company, and not required for a trading purpose. This is to prevent 'money box' companies from obtaining business asset taper relief.

What is 'significant' in this context is generally regarded as being either 20% of net assets, or 20% of income.

If the cash was retained for a trading purpose there would in any case be no problem, however it would not otherwise be advisable to build up large cash balances within the company that could be regarded as an 'investment activity'.

13.8 How Many Shares Should be Issued?

This is entirely a matter for you as the prospective shareholders and directors of the company. In general I would advise that a share capital of at least £100 is retained. This will then allow for easier distribution of shares.

One common situation would be for director shareholders to wish to reduce the size of their estates for IHT reasons. If share capital of only £2 was issued this would be more complex than if £100 of share capital was originally subscribed for. The shareholders could then transfer 5 or 10 shares to family members, (hopefully claiming full capital gains tax and inheritance tax reliefs in addition!).

Chapter 14

Incorporating an Existing Business

14.1 Income Tax & Capital Allowances

The transfer of an unincorporated business to a company results in a "cessation of trade". Choosing the correct day on which to cease trading can provide you with a significant opportunity to defer your final income tax payments.

By delaying the incorporation by two or three months, in certain circumstances it is possible to defer paying the final tax bill for the unincorporated business by up to 12 months.

A cessation of trade also normally results in "balancing adjustments" to capital allowances.

It is important to understand that the purpose of the capital allowances legislation is to provide tax relief for the total cost of an asset *over its lifetime*. Therefore suppose that an asset is acquired for £10,000 and after three years, tax relief of £5,000 has been obtained through the capital allowance system. If in year four the asset is sold for £8,000, there would normally be a balancing charge of £3,000.

The "loss" to the business was effectively £2,000 because the asset was bought for £10,000 and sold for £8,000. As tax relief of £5,000 has been given, the additional £3,000 is clawed back. This amount would then be "added back" in calculating profits.

However, if the disposal of the assets of the business is to a company controlled by the sole trader or partners, a form of relief is available to avoid these balancing charges.

It is possible for the business to transfer the plant and machinery to the company at its open market value and for the potential balancing charge to be avoided by making a joint election under the 'succession' provisions contained in the capital allowances legislation.

The effect of the election is to treat the business as transferring the plant and machinery to the company at a price which produces no balancing allowance/charge (in other words, at the tax written down value at which the business holds the assets). The company's capital allowances are calculated as though it had always owned the transferred plant and machinery. There is therefore a continuity of capital allowances, with no balancing adjustments.

Points to note about the election are:

- The original partners/traders will not be entitled to capital allowances for the period of account in which the incorporation takes place.

- No first year allowances can be claimed in the cessation period. These allowances are given at a rate of 40% in the accounting period of purchase for general plant and machinery and 100% for other specified assets, eg, energy saving plant and machinery and computers purchased before 31 March 2004. The 40% first year allowance rate has been increased in the 2004 budget to 50% for expenditure incurred between 1 April 2004 and 1 April 2005.

Therefore if there is considerable capital expenditure which would otherwise qualify for first year allowances, it may be worthwhile drawing up accounts to an earlier date, so that the actual final cessation period is small. It would then be possible to obtain first year allowances/writing down allowances in the penultimate period.

14.2 Capital Gains Tax

Often the key consideration when disposing of a business is the amount of capital gains tax payable. The good news is CGT can usually be avoided completely when you incorporate an existing sole trader business or partnership.

The disposal of an unincorporated business is treated for taxation purposes as a disposal of the assets employed in the business. It will, therefore, be necessary to prepare computations of the chargeable gains and allowable losses in respect of all chargeable assets including:

- Goodwill
- Land & buildings
- Fixed plant & machinery
- Tangible moveable property with a market value in excess of £6,000 (this usually applies to large moveable pieces of plant and machinery).

How the Gain is Calculated

A typical capital gains tax calculation looks like this:

	£
Proceeds (1)	X
<u>Less</u>:Incidental costs of disposal (2)	(X)
<u>Less</u>:Acquisition cost (3)	(X)
<u>Less</u>:Incidental costs of acquisition	(X)
<u>Less</u>:Enhancement expenditure (4)	<u>(X)</u>
Unindexed gain	**X**
Less:Indexation allowance (5)	(X)
Less:Reliefs	(X)
Less:Annual exemption	<u>(X)</u>
Chargeable gain	**X**

<u>Notes:</u>

(1) The disposal proceeds will, in the majority of cases, be the market value of the assets at the date of incorporation.

However, a disposal is deemed to take place at market value in certain circumstances, for example when a disposal is made between connected persons, or the transfer is by way of a gift.

(2) Incidental costs of disposal/acquisition include legal fees relating to the disposal/purchase, stamp duty, auctioneer's fees etc.

(3) The cost of the asset is the original cost of the asset. There are special rules for assets acquired before 31 March 1982 and 5 April 1965.

(4) Enhancement expenditure is expenditure incurred in improving the value of the asset that has not obtained tax relief in another form. It must also be reflected in the state and nature of the asset at the date of disposal.

So for example, expenditure incurred in refurbishing and extending a restaurant property prior to sale would be likely to qualify as enhancement expenditure.

(5) Indexation allowance is another allowable deduction. This is intended to provide a measure of relief for the effect of inflation. It is calculated by using the Retail Prices Index (RPI) and is computed according to the following formula:

$$\frac{\text{RPI at date of disposal} - \text{RPI at date of purchase}}{\text{RPI at date of purchase}}$$

this would then be rounded to 3 decimal places.

For a disposal by an individual, indexation allowance will only apply until April 1998. After this date any disposals will attract indexation up to April 1998 and *taper relief* for the remaining period until disposal (see below).

In the case of a rapidly expanding business, the value of the goodwill may be substantial. Similarly, land & property that had been owned for a significant period could also generate large gains.

Reliefs

There are two main methods of avoiding a capital gains tax charge when you incorporate a business. These are:

- Incorporation relief

- Gift relief

Incorporation relief provides for a form of 'rollover' relief if ALL the assets of the business are transferred as a going concern to the company in exchange for shares issued by the company.

Gift relief provides for a form of 'holdover' relief where individuals transfer business assets to the company for a consideration which is less than the market value of the assets. Both of these reliefs are mutually exclusive.

We shall look at these two methods in further detail below, as it is important to fully assess the capital gains tax position when you incorporate.

However, before we do this it is important to talk a little about the effect of taper relief, in particular business asset taper relief.

This is a potentially generous relief and can result in the effective capital gains tax rate for a higher rate taxpayer being as low as 10%.

Taper relief applies where assets are disposed of after 5 April 1998. It reduces the amount of the chargeable gain according to the length of time that the asset has been held after 5 April 1998.

The amount of taper relief depends initially on the nature of the asset. Secondly, having determined the nature of the asset, rules need to be applied to determine the length of ownership and thus the rate of taper relief.

Taper relief is always the last relief to be deducted, and therefore if a gain is deferred by using incorporation or gift relief, no taper relief would be given (as there would be no gain!). The important point to understand is that an incorporation would have the effect of "restarting the taper relief clock". As the amount of taper relief given depends on the length of the period of ownership, if the shares in the company were to be disposed of within two years of incorporation, a significantly higher rate of capital gains tax may be payable on the disposal, than if the company had remained as a sole trader business.

Example

John had owned his trading business since 1985 and had plans to retire in June 2004. He decided to incorporate his business in September 2003. Assuming the assets qualified for the higher business asset rate of taper relief, if he had remained as an unincorporated business he would obtain 75% taper relief on a disposal in June 2004 (in other words, 75% reduction in the chargeable gain after indexation).

As he incorporated his business in September 2003 he would obtain no taper relief as he would not have owned the shares for the minimum 1 year period at the date of disposal in June 2004.

The ownership period for business asset taper relief has now been reduced to two years. Therefore, provided the shares are disposed of more than two years after incorporation, the ownership criterion will be satisfied. However, this area should be looked at carefully. Taper relief has many potential traps, the only purpose of which is to trap the unwary! You should take professional advice to ensure that your shares will qualify for business asset status.

Incorporation relief

The capital gains tax liability on the incorporation of a business can be deferred in whole or in part provided that:

- All the assets of the business (excluding cash if desired) are transferred to the company; and

- The business is transferred as a going concern; and

- The business is transferred wholly or partly in exchange for shares issued by the company to the person(s) transferring the business.

It is the Inland Revenue's view that most commercial businesses will qualify for relief, although they have stated that they would resist granting this relief on the transfer of a "passive" holding of investments or an investment property.

This reinforces the point made at the beginning of the guide that certain reliefs are given only to trading businesses.

Example

Ethan commenced trading in May 1987 as a builders merchant. His business has been successful and he now wishes to incorporate by forming BM Ltd.

A summary of the assets of the business, including current market value is as follows:

	Market value £'000	Book value £'000	Cost £'000
Land & buildings	500	150	150
Plant & equipment (each item valued at less than £6,000)	50	50	125
Goodwill	200	-	-
Stock	100	100	-
Cash	60	60	-
Less: Trade creditors	(150)	(150)	-
Total	760	210	275

If Ethan incorporates his business wholly in exchange for shares, the following chargeable gains will arise:

Land & buildings	£'000
Market value	500
Cost	(150)
Indexation	(90)
Gain	260

Goodwill	
Market value	200
Cost	-
Indexation	-
Gain	200

Total chargeable gains: £260,000 + £200,000 = £460,000.

As BM Ltd will take over all the assets (except cash) and liabilities, shares will be issued with a CGT base cost of £760,000 - £60,000 = £700,000.

The effect of the incorporation relief is to reduce the base cost of the shares by the amount of the chargeable gains to be rolled over. In this case the revised base cost of the shares would be £700,000 - £460,000 = £240,000. This would have the effect of effectively rolling over the gain arising on incorporation until the shares in the company were disposed of.

If there are assets owned by the business that are not used for trading purposes, eg investments or land which is surplus to business requirements and is let to various tenants, it would be necessary to not transfer such assets to the company as they are not assets used in the business and any chargeable gains arising on the transfer would be unlikely to qualify for the relief.

It should be noted that if the chargeable gain on incorporation exceeds the cost of the shares issued to the owners of the unincorporated business, the excess gain is subject to capital gains tax as normal and incorporation relief would not be available.

The disadvantage of incorporation relief is that ALL of the assets of the business must be transferred to the company. This is likely to be expensive in terms of stamp duty. However, if assets are retained in order to save stamp duty a capital gains tax charge may then arise on all the chargeable assets transferred to the company.

Another condition for incorporation relief is that the business is transferred in exchange for shares issued by the company to the person transferring the business. If the shares were therefore issued to the son of the person disposing of the business, this would restrict the availability of relief as the son would not be a proprietor of the sole trader business.

If the father were to transfer all assets in exchange for shares issued to solely him, incorporation relief would be available. The subsequent transfer of shares to the son, however, would be both a potentially exempt transfer (PET) for inheritance tax, and a disposal for capital gains tax purposes.

Note, that incorporation relief effectively deducts the gain on incorporation from the base cost of the shares issued. Therefore an immediate transfer to the son would realise part of the gain deferred on incorporation.

This is where gift relief comes to the rescue.

Gift relief

The gift relief provisions were not originally intended for business incorporations. However, this route has proved to be successful and in certain cases has significant benefits over the use of incorporation relief. Many incorporations today use gift relief particularly in order to obtain the use of a tax free loan account with the company.

The basic effect of gift relief is that any gains on the assets are held over against the cost of the assets to the company. For example, if a building was transferred that had a market value of £100,000, and a gain was to arise of £30,000, the company would hold the asset at a base cost of £70,000.

What happens with this amount that is 'held over'?

The amount held over is reduced from the cost of the asset to the company. Therefore, if the company were to subsequently dispose of the goodwill (eg on a disposal of the trade and assets), the proportion of the gain held over would in effect become chargeable.

It is worthwhile noting that should the shareholders decide to dispose of the shares in the company within the next 2 years, the capital gains tax charge would be substantially higher than if the business was left unincorporated and the trade and assets were disposed of.

This is because on incorporation the taper relief 'clock' starts again, and you and the other shareholders would need to own the shares for at least 2 years to obtain maximum 75% business asset taper relief.

Example

If Ethan had decided to incorporate his business using gift relief, it would be possible for him to personally retain the land and buildings which could be let to the company. This would enable the property to be protected from creditors on a liquidation and would allow cash to be extracted from the company as rent with no national insurance having to be paid (remember national insurance is only payable on earned income, not investment income).

The goodwill would be transferred along with the trade to the company. The effect would be:

Goodwill	£
Market value	200,000
Cost	-
Indexation	-
Gift relief	(200,000)
Gain	NIL

BM Ltd would therefore hold the goodwill with a deemed acquisition cost of nil.

It is possible to elect to dispense with the valuing of goodwill in accordance with an Inland Revenue statement of practice. On a straightforward gift, there would be no need to value the goodwill at incorporation as the gift relief claim would ensure that the company would always obtain the base cost of the transferring trader.

Since April 2000, the shares in the company are likely to qualify for business asset taper relief as all unlisted shares in trading companies qualify as business assets from this date.

Note that where a trading asset is gifted with no disposal proceeds, any gain would be entirely deferred under gift relief.

However, this is unusual. Usually, an asset is partially gifted, with some disposal proceeds being received or more commonly, left outstanding on a loan account.

How this works is that you are claiming gift relief to 'hold over' the gain. However, because the goodwill is not actually gifted, the gift relief is restricted to leave an amount of gain equivalent to the disposal proceeds. The basic theory being that gains can be fully deferred when gifted as there will be no disposal proceeds with which to pay any capital gains tax. However, where they are part sold, there will be some disposal proceeds, and as such part of the gain will be chargeable.

The disposal proceeds would then establish the loan account, which allows cash to be extracted free of tax and national insurance – the establishment of the loan account is considered shortly.

Gift relief procedure

The procedure that would need to be adopted is as follows:

1. A company is formed and a small number of shares would be issued for cash to the owners of the business.

2. At the date of incorporation the owners of the business enter into an agreement with the company whereby:
   - The goodwill of the business is sold to the company for a nominal figure, and
   - All the other trading assets are sold at their book values.

3. The consideration for the assets transferred is satisfied wholly by cash or left on loan account. No more shares would be issued.

4. The parties sign a joint declaration to hold over any chargeable gains arising.

5. The debts of the original business are normally not transferred and would instead be collected by the original owners.

This route has two main advantages over incorporation relief:

- It is usual to transfer goodwill for a nominal sum.

- A sizeable loan account can be established if the consideration in point (3) above is left outstanding. This can then be withdrawn from the company free of tax and national insurance.

It is this loan account that is advantageous to many business owners. Remember what the difference is here between incorporation relief and gift relief. Incorporation relief applies where all the assets are gifted in exchange for shares. There will therefore be no loan account with this.

Gift relief involves selling business assets to a company at less than their market value. If the assets were sold at full value, there would be no gift relief, and a gain would arise. However, the loan account would then be the amount of the disposal proceeds. If you are willing to take a small capital gains tax hit now, you could therefore reap the benefits of the larger loan account later on (see the example below).

Alternatively, gift relief can be used to reduce or eliminate any capital gains tax charge, yet still ensure that a (smaller) loan account is established. This loan account can be withdrawn by the person disposing of the business free of national insurance and income tax.

This is advantageous to many people considering incorporating a business. In fact one Inspector of Taxes I recently spoke to suggested that all incorporations should attempt to make use of the tax free loan account.

Can other directors use the loan account?

No, as the loan account is simply the disposal proceeds for the assets sold to the company, the cash would need to be extracted by the person(s) who actually sold the business.

If there is another person who is a director (eg a spouse or adult child) one option would be for them to have their own loan account, and for this to be cleared by the disposing person's loan account. As it is a gift of cash there would be no capital gains tax implications, although for inheritance this would be a potentially exempt transfer, and as such provided the parent survived for at least seven years, this would be completely excluded from his estate.

Example
Peter sold the goodwill of his sole trader business to his newly formed company Peter Limited for £100,000. Peter did not claim any gift relief.

The gain arising on this was £100,000, however, after full business asset taper relief and the annual exemption, the gain was approximately £17,000. He paid CGT of £6,800.

The company did not have the funds to pay Peter his £100,000 and therefore left this outstanding. In its accounts this would be shown as a creditor.

Peter can then use this as a way of getting cash out of the company free of tax. As the repayment of a loan this is NOT classed as income in his hands.

On the formation of the company Peter's son Patrick, subscribed for some shares. Peter is keen to reduce his tax charge, and would like Patrick to benefit from the loan account.

One method would be for Patrick to withdraw sums from the company and, before the balance exceeds £5,000, arrange for Peter's loan account to clear Patrick's. This could either be via a book transfer (for any bookkeepers out there Dr Peter's loan account and Cr Patrick's loan account).

The creation of a loan account and the use of gift relief to restrict having to pay any capital gains tax now is most common with goodwill.

For the 2004/2005 tax year, an established business could potentially dispose of goodwill to the company for £32,800 without any CGT implications.

Example
During 2004/2005 Jack and Jill decide to incorporate their trading business which they have run for the last 10 years. The business goodwill is valued at £90,000, but they decide to sell it to the company for £32,800 each, holding over any gain arising. The capital gains tax position is as follows:

	Jack £	Jill £
Goodwill - market value	45,000	45,000
Less:Held over gain (restricted)	(12,200)	(12,200)
Sale proceeds	32,800	32,800
Less:Taper relief (75%)	(24,600)	(24,600)
	8,200	8,200
Less: Annual exemption (2004/05)	(8,200)	(8,200)
Chargeable gains	Nil	Nil

Both Jack and Jill can then withdraw up to £32,800 each from the company with no tax or national insurance implications!

As always the allocation of any proceeds in the sale and purchase agreement should be accurate and on a *bona fide* basis, particularly as the Inland Revenue can challenge such apportionments.

Valuation of goodwill

For capital gains tax purposes, the computation is of the 'market value' of business goodwill as a separate asset.

Market value is defined in the tax legislation as being 'the price which (the asset) might reasonably be expected to fetch on a sale in the open market'.

Therefore, in short, goodwill is the difference between the market value of the business, less the value of any other assets that the purchaser would obtain. It is this difference that is the goodwill of the business.

There are numerous ways of valuing goodwill. One option would be to instruct a business valuer to value the business and any goodwill. You should also identify similar businesses for sale and compare their prices. Similarly, you could discount the value of future income receipts from the business using a suitable discount rate.

Many transfer agents will provide free valuation services. It would be worthwhile taking them up on this and there are numerous business and goodwill valuation software solutions that will provide a good starting point for figures.

Note that where gift relief is being claimed, care needs to be taken as to the order of events. The shares must be issued prior to the incorporation. This is because any amount received for the transfer of assets would reduce the availability of gift relief.

That's why incorporation relief and gift relief are mutually exclusive - under incorporation relief, the shares are issued in consideration of the transfer of assets.

Transfer of cash in the bank

What about any cash that is retained in the sole trader's bank account?

This could be transferred or gifted to the company. However, one option would be to retain the cash and separately loan this to the company (draw up a suitable loan agreement). This would then be added to the loan account and be extracted without a tax or national insurance charge.

Again, interest could be charged if wished which would be free of national insurance, although income tax would still be charged.

Trading stock

Trading stock would not be subject to capital gains tax rules on a disposal.

On a transfer to the company, any charge would be under income tax. There are special provisions that deal with the transfer of stock to 'connected parties' such as your own company.

The normal connected person's rule imposes an arm's length value for the stock transferred between them, and the person incorporating the business would therefore be deemed to have disposed of the stock at market value and the company would have acquired it at market value. This could however cause substantial unrealised profits to be charged to tax on incorporation.

The tax legislation allows for an election to be made to substitute a different value as opposed to the market value.

There are a number of conditions to be satisfied for a valid election, as follows:

- The arm's length value is more than the acquisition value of the stock, and the price actually paid for it, and

- Both the person transferring the stock and the company make an election to Inland Revenue. The election must be made within two tax years after the end of the chargeable period in which the trade is discontinued.

The value substituted would then be the greater of the acquisition value and the price actually received for it.

Therefore, assuming stock was transferred to the company at book value, provided the market value was in excess of this and a valid election was made and accepted by the Inland Revenue, no trading profit would arise. The company would then hold the stock at the original book value, and any profit would then be taxed in the company's hands on disposal of the stock.

The disposal consideration for the book value of the stock could be either settled in cash or left outstanding in a loan account.

Example
Patrick is transferring his business to a company. Included in the transfer will be some of the stock (widgets) of his sole trader business.

The widgets have an original cost of £5,000, but their current market value is £10,000.

Patrick is therefore looking at a potential profit of £5,000 on transfer. This would be subject to income tax and assuming he is a 40% taxpayer, income tax of £2,000 would be payable, even though he has not actually received any consideration with which to satisfy the liability.

However, Patrick would be able to transfer the widgets to the company at £5,000, and make the appropriate election. No profit would arise on transfer, and assuming the company later sold the widgets for £10,000, the £5,000 profit would arise in the company.

14.3 Inheritance Tax (IHT)

In the vast majority of cases the incorporation of a business will not have any IHT implications as IHT is based on the "diminution in value" principle. This basically means that IHT applies where an individual's estate (his assets less liabilities) has reduced. In the case of an incorporation, the value of shares will usually equal the value of the interest in the business transferred to the company. There will therefore be no reduction in the value of the estate and no gift arises for IHT purposes.

On the death of an individual, there is an IHT relief called business property relief ("BPR") that may apply so as to completely remove certain assets from the estate and from the IHT net.

It is worthwhile noting the following points in relation to BPR on an incorporation:

- All shareholdings in the new company will usually qualify for 100% BPR (provided the company is a trading company). Although it is required that the asset has been owned for two years, the period of ownership of the original business will be taken into account for this purpose.

- Partners who own land/buildings used by a business partnership would normally qualify for 50% BPR. In the case of an individual owning such assets for the use of a company, it is only the controlling shareholder that would obtain 50% BPR (although it is acceptable to combine the interests of husband and wife to determine whether either of them controls the company).

Example
John, one of the partners in the Bloggs & Co partnership, owns the partnership property which is leased to the business. The partnership pays a full market rental.

In the event of John's death, the property used by the partnership would qualify for 50% BPR.

If the partnership were incorporated, and John was issued with 3,000 ordinary shares with his fellow partner receiving 7,000 shares, John would be a minority shareholder.

Assuming the property remained with John, he would not be entitled to any Business Property Relief were he to die whilst still owning the asset.

14.4 VAT

The general rule is that the disposal of goods forming part of the assets of a business is a supply made in the course of the business and therefore VAT will be chargeable on the sale of fixtures, fittings, plant and machinery and stock. Customs and Excise also treat disposals of goodwill as taxable supplies.

However, there is one key relief available which applies where the transfer of the business is a "transfer of a going concern".

The conditions required to be satisfied are:

- There is a transfer of a business or a part of a business capable of separate operation.

- The transfer must be of a going concern (TOGC), in other words, there must be no significant break in trading.

- The transferee must carry on the same kind of business as the transferor.

- The transferee must already be or must become a VAT registered trader.

It should also be noted that there are special provisions that apply to TOGC treatment where a property that is being transferred is a supply subject to VAT.

Where the ownership of the business is transferred to the company, it is possible for the trader and company to jointly apply on VAT form 68 for the company to take over the transferor's original VAT registration, provided that:

- The registration of the original business is to be cancelled from the date of the transfer.

- The new business is not already registered, but is liable or entitled to be registered.

The effect of a successful application would be that the company stands in the shoes of the transferor and would therefore take over the VAT rights and obligations of the transferor.

14.5 Stamp Duty

Stamp duty has been reformed from December 2003. A new tax known as Stamp Duty Land Tax ('SDLT') is now charged in a similar way to the old stamp duty on land transferred.

If any land is to be transferred to the company, the SDLT implications will therefore need to be considered.

The rates of SDLT have basically remained the same as the old stamp duty rates, except for a new £150,000 threshold for non-residential property.

On residential property the rates for purchases are:

Consideration	%
Up to £60,000	0
More than £60,000 and up to £250,000	1
More than £250,000 and up to £500,000	3
More than £500,000	4

On non-residential property the rates for purchases are:

Consideration	%
Up to £150,000	0
More than £150,000 and up to £250,000	1
More than £250,000 and up to £500,000	3
More than £500,000	4

The exemption for non residential property with a value of up to £150,000 is a useful addition, and will exempt many small businesses who wish to transfer their business premises, although it is fair to say that stamp duty would not have been a key consideration – the corporation tax and capital gains tax implications are arguably the most important.

Many of the changes are really just a case of bringing stamp duty into the 21st century.

The appeals procedure has been changed and brought more into line with income tax and capital gains tax. In particular, SDLT is a tax on transactions as opposed to documents, reducing opportunities to avoid the tax charge. If you plan to transfer the lease of your business premises, you should take professional advice, as there are some complex provisions regarding the SDLT charge on leases.

There is an exemption from stamp duty on the sale or transfer of goodwill upon incorporation, in respect of documents executed after 22 April 2002.

This makes the sale of goodwill to a company upon incorporation (as opposed to a gift) potentially more attractive. The sale proceeds could be left outstanding as a loan to the company, and withdrawn without further tax consequences as described in 14.2.

In the past debtors used to often be retained by the sole trader in order to avoid stamp duty. However, stamp duty is no longer charged on the transfer of debtors, and they could therefore be transferred to the company.

Even if they were transferred note that the receipt of money from a debtor would not usually be charged to tax. Under the accruals basis of accounting, the sale will have already been recorded and taxed in the sole traders accounts (Dr Debtors, Cr Sales). The receipt of cash by the company would then not impact on the profit and loss account, being only a balance sheet transaction (Dr Cash, Cr Debtors).

Chapter 15

Incorporation Checklist

The precise procedures to follow when setting up a company will depend to a large extent on the particular trade/business you are undertaking.

As a guide the following actions should be taken:

- Check that no trade rules prohibit you trading as a limited company.

- Consider the timing of incorporation. In particular, if cash flow is important note that the date of cessation can impact heavily on the final income tax assessments.

- Consider:
  1. The value of goodwill.
  2. Whether and how to avoid capital gains tax.
  3. Shareholdings, and appointing directors and company secretary.
  4. What assets are to go into the company.

- Once you've formed the company and have the company number:
  1. Open a new bank account.
  2. Consider VAT registration or transfer of registration.
  3. Get new stationery.

- Consider whether to have a formal sale document or just heads of agreement.

- Consider VAT implications - is there a transfer of a going concern?

- Draw up sales agreement and if necessary get it stamped.

- Inform everyone concerned (customers, suppliers, the taxman etc).

- Put any legal transfer of land and buildings into motion.

- Commence trading in company name.

- If you used holdover relief to avoid capital gains tax on goodwill, submit holdover relief claim.

- Set up new accounting system.

- When submitting tax returns, do not forget cessation rules or CGT computations.

Chapter 16

Offshore Tax Planning

Although not directly relevant to many of you considering incorporating your business, it's worthwhile giving an overview of the various offshore tax rules.

The first point to note when looking at overseas tax planning is that it is *residence* that is all important. Both companies and individuals have residence in one or more countries and it is this residence that primarily determines liability to UK taxes.

A company is regarded as a UK resident if:

- It is a UK incorporated company, or
- Its *central management and control* is in the UK.

Therefore, where a UK registered company is used, the company would automatically be UK resident. The effect of this is that it is subject to UK corporation tax on its worldwide income and gains.

By contrast, an offshore company that is centrally managed and controlled from overseas would only be charged to UK corporation tax on its UK income. Any overseas income and all gains would be outside the scope of UK corporation tax. (Note that gains arising from assets used in a UK trade would still be charged to UK corporation tax).

Some people try and live in the UK, yet argue that the central management and control of their company is undertaken overseas.

Various legal cases have indicated that where the board of directors meet and give proper consideration to any transactions the company undertakes constitutes the central management and control. There is a risk that proper procedures may not be followed and in such cases Inland Revenue may argue that the company is run by the controlling shareholder in the UK. In these circumstances the company would be classed as UK resident and subject to UK corporation tax.

As regards individuals, there is no formal legal definition of 'residence'. Inland Revenue's practice - based on a mixture of statute and court decisions - is to regard you as resident in the UK during a tax year if :

- You spend 183 days or more in the UK during the tax year, or

- Although here for less than 183 days, you have spent more than 90 days per year in the country over the past four years (taken as an average). You will then be classed as UK resident from the fifth year.

Note that for capital gains tax purposes, there are special provisions that may require you to remain overseas for at least 5 tax years to avoid UK capital gains tax.

UK resident individuals are subject to UK income tax and capital gains tax on their worldwide income and gains, whereas non-resident individuals are only subject to UK income tax on their UK income and gains arising from assets used in a UK trade.

How does this affect you?

There are plenty of ways that the offshore dimension could affect your tax planning.

1) Assume you operate a UK business and want to dispose of this to avoiding UK capital gains tax. One option would be to become non resident, and dispose of the business?

Wrong! The disposal would continue to be within the charge to UK capital gains tax, as the various assets disposed of would be classed as part of a UK trade.

A method to side step this would be to incorporate your business. By transferring your business to a company, you now own the shares in the company, and the company owns the business.

You could then become non resident and dispose of the shares, as opposed to the assets. Provided the purchaser has no objection, and you satisfy the various non-residency requirements, your disposal would be exempt from UK capital gains tax, as a disposal of an asset which is not used in a UK trade.

2) What about incorporating your business into an offshore company?

This would be fine provided the company was within the charge to UK corporation tax (ie UK resident). If you argued that the company was non resdident and outside the scope of UK capital gains tax the Inland Revenue would not be too happy about allowing a deferral of gains on incorporation where a future disposal would be outside the scope of UK tax. Therefore gift relief would be restricted.

3) What if you went to live overseas – any opportunities there?

If you became non resident, this opens up more options to minimise UK tax.

You could pay yourself dividends from your UK company, effectively free of UK income tax, as any higher rate tax is restricted and the notional tax credit is deemed to satisfy any basic rate liability. This could be a useful mechanism for extracting cash from the company – build up funds in the company over a number of years and pay a large dividend during the tax year of non residence, free of UK income tax!

(Note there would be other additional implications to consider here).

When compared to an unincorporated business, this looks very favourable, as profits from a UK trade would be fully charged to UK income tax, just as for a UK resident individual.

However, when using a company, although corporation tax is still payable by the company, this is significantly less than the income tax charge for a sole trader/partner, and no personal tax liability!

For a more detailed look at the offshore opportunities available, see our recent publication *Non Resident & Offshore Tax Planning* available from the Taxcafe.co.uk website.

Chapter 17

Conclusion

There are a number of issues to consider on the incorporation of a business, including, both taxation and commercial implications.

The initial step should be to consider whether there are any advantages to be gained from incorporation. The use of salaries/dividends and directors loan accounts should be carefully evaluated against the likely profitability of the company.

Once a decision to incorporate has been made, the question then is how to incorporate and to ensure that the deferral reliefs are obtained. The structure of an incorporation will usually be driven by the vendor's requirements in the context of these reliefs. In recent years, the gift relief route has often been preferred as it can secure significant stamp duty savings and can facilitate the creation of a loan account in the purchase company that can be repaid tax free.

All proposed business incorporations should also be considered in terms of the taper relief position, particularly as the incorporation will restart the taper relief "clock" and could result in significant additional capital gains tax, if a disposal of the shares in the company is anticipated shortly after the incorporation.

Please note that the issues contained in this guide are intended for guidance only and professional advice should always be taken with regard to your particular circumstances.

Need Affordable & Expert Tax Planning Advice?

Try Our Unique Question & Answer Service

The purpose of this guide is to provide you with detailed guidance on the pros and cons of running your business through a company.

Ultimately you may want to take further action or obtain advice personal to your circumstances.

Taxcafe.co.uk has a unique online tax advice service that provides access to highly qualified tax professionals at an affordable rate.

No matter how complex your question, we will provide you with detailed tax planning guidance through this service. The cost is just £69.95.

To find out more go to **www.taxcafe.co.uk** and click the Tax Questions button.

Pay Less Tax!

... with help from Taxcafe's unique tax guides, software and Q&A service

All products available online at **www.taxcafe.co.uk**

➢ **How to Avoid Property Tax.** Essential reading for property investors who want to know all the tips and tricks to follow to pay less tax on their property profits.

➢ **Using a Property Company to Save Tax.** How to massively increase your profits by using a property company... plus all the traps to avoid.

➢ **How to Avoid Inheritance Tax.** A-Z of inheritance tax planning, with clear explanations & numerous examples. Covers simple & sophisticated tax planning.

➢ **Non Resident & Offshore Tax Planning.** How to exploit non resident tax status to reduce your tax bill, plus advice on using offshore trusts and companies.

➢ **Incorporate & Save Tax.** Everything you need to know about the tax benefits of using a company to run your business.

➢ **Bonus vs Dividends.** Shows how shareholder/directors of companies can save thousands in tax by choosing the optimal mix of bonus and dividends.

➢ **Selling a Business.** A potential minefield with numerous traps to avoid but significant tax saving opportunities.

➢ **How to Claim Tax Credits.** Even families with higher incomes can make successful tax credit claims. This guide shows how much you can claim and how to go about it.

➢ **Property Capital Gains Tax Calculator.** Unique software that performs complex capital gains tax calculations in seconds.

➢ **Fast Tax Advice.** We offer a unique Tax Question Service. Answers from highly qualified specialist tax advisers. Just click the Tax Questions button on our site.

Essential Property Investment Guides

...written by leading experts and packed with tips & tricks of the trade

All products available online at **www.taxcafe.co.uk**

- ➤ **An Insider's Guide to Successful Property Investing.** Little-known secrets of successful property investors. A "must read" for anyone interested in making big profits and avoiding costly mistakes.

- ➤ **An Insider's Guide to Successful Property Investing - Part II.** How the experts make millions by using simple but clever techniques to find, buy, manage and sell property.

- ➤ **No Money Down Property Millions.** Written by a wealthy property investor, this entertaining and brilliantly clever guide shows you how to invest in property without using any of your own money.

- ➤ **The Successful Landlord's Handbook.** Definitive guide for Buy to Let investors. Covers: sourcing cheap property, using borrowed money to earn big capital gains, finding quality tenants, earning high rents, legal traps, letting agents, and lots more...

- ➤ **63 Common Defects in Investment Property & How to Spot Them.** With full colour illustrations, this unique guide will save you thousands by steering you clear of no-hope property investments and towards bargain-priced gems.

- ➤ **Property Auctions Bargains.** One of the best-kept secrets of successful property investors is to buy at rock-bottom prices at auction. This A-Z guide tells you everything you need to know.

www.taxcafe.co.uk

DISCLAIMER BY TAXCAFE UK LIMITED AND L J HADNUM

1.   Please note that this Tax Guide is intended as general guidance only for individual readers and does NOT constitute accountancy, tax, investment or other professional advice. Further general tax guidance on circumstances not covered in this Tax Guide can be obtained through the TAXCafe™ online "Question and Answer" Service which is available at www.taxcafe.co.uk. Taxcafe UK Limited and LJ Hadnum accepts no responsibility or liability for loss which may arise from reliance on information contained in this Tax Guide.

2.   Please note that tax legislation, the law and practices by government and regulatory authorities (eg Inland Revenue) are constantly changing and the information contained in this Tax Guide is only correct as at the date of publication. We therefore recommend that for accountancy, tax, investment or other professional advice, you consult a suitably qualified accountant, tax specialist, independent financial adviser, or other professional adviser. Please also note that your personal circumstances may vary from the general examples given in this Tax Guide and your professional adviser will be able to give specific advice based on your personal circumstances.

3.   This Tax Guide covers UK taxation only and any references to "tax" or "taxation" in this Tax Guide, unless the contrary is expressly stated, refers to UK taxation only. Please note that references to the "UK" do not include the Channel Islands or the Isle of Man. Foreign tax implications are beyond the scope of this Tax Guide.

4.   Whilst in an effort to be helpful, this Tax Guide may refer to general guidance on matters other than UK taxation. Taxcafe UK Limited and LJ Hadnum are not experts in these matters and do not accept any responsibility or liability for loss which may arise from reliance on such information contained in this Tax Guide.

5.   Please note that Taxcafe UK Limited has relied wholly upon the expertise of the author in the preparation of the content of this Tax Guide. The author is not an employee of Taxcafe UK Limited but has been selected by Taxcafe UK Limited using reasonable care and skill to write the content of this Tax Guide.

Printed in the United Kingdom
by Lightning Source UK Ltd.
100722UKS00002B/1-123